Effectiveness o
Procedure in t

Tinsy Ramakrishnan

Contents

List of Tables

List of Figures

1. INTRODUCTION 1

1.1 An overview of Autism 2
   1.1.1 Epidemiology 3
   1.1.2 Characteristics and Diagnosis 5
   1.1.3 Etiological perspective 8
   1.1.4 Neurological basis of Autism 15
   1.1.5 Management 20
      1.1.5.1 Medical Management 21
      1.1.5.2 Educational Intervention 21
      1.1.5.3 Family support 27

1.2 Statement of the problem 28

1.3 Variables of the study 28
   1.3.1 Multisensory Stimulation 28
   1.3.2 Dependent Variables 32
      1.3.2.1 Motor skills 33
      1.3.2.2 Communication skills 34
      1.3.2.3 Cognitive skills 35

1.4 Hypotheses 35

1.5 Method 36

1.5.1 Participants 37
1.5.2 Tools used for measurement... 37
1.5.3 Procedure 38
1.5.4 Analysis of data 39
1.6 Outline of the thesis 39

2. REVIEW OF RELATED LITERATURE 41

3. METHOD 55

3.1 Design of the study 56
   3.1.1 Single Subject Research 56
   3.1.2 Multiple Baseline Design.. 59
3.2 Participants and setting... 60
   3.2.1 The participants 62
   3.2.2 Observer in the study 63
   3.2.3 Setting and time 63
3.3 Tools used for the study 64
   3.3.1 Vineland's Social Maturity Scale (VSMS)........................ 64
   3.3.2 Childhood Autism Rating Scale (CARS)......................... 64
   3.3.3 The Sensory Integration Inventory (SII-R)..................... 64
   3.3.4 Curriculum Guide for autistic children 66
3.4 Procedure.. 66
   3.4.1 Case history and Assessment 66

  3.4.1.1 Participant no.1 - Aman 67

  3.4.1.2 Participant no.2 - Sam 69

  3.4.1.3 Participant no.3 - John 72

  3.4.1.4 Participant no.4 - Roshan 74

 3.4.2 Data collection 76

  3.4.2.1 Measuring Behavior 77

   3.4.2.1.1 Magnitude: Measuring the response strength 78

 3.4.3 The behavior modification program and scoring 81

  3.4.3.1 Participant no.1 - Aman 82

  3.4.3.2 Participant no.2 - Sam 117

 3.4.4 Reliability of the procedure 147

3.5 Statistical Approaches 148

 3.5.1 Inter observer Agreement 148

 3.5.2 Visual Analysis 149

  3.5.2.1 The behavior modification program 150

   3.5.2.1.1 Line graphs 151

   3.5.2.1.2 Effect size 152

  3.5.2.2 Pre post test score comparison of the sensory profile. 154

4. RESULTS AND DISCUSSION 156

4.1 Inter Observer Agreement 158

 4.1.1 Participant no.1 - Aman 158

 4.1.2 Participant no.2 - Sam 159

4.2 Visual analysis 161
4.2.1 The Behavior ModificationProgram 161
4.2.1.1 Participant no.1 - Aman 161
4.2.1.1.1 First tier of activities.. 161
4.2.1.1.2 Second tier of activities 164
4.2.1.1.3 Third tier of activities 165
4.2.1.1.4 Fourth tier of activities 167
4.2.1.1.5 Fifth tier of activities 168
4.2.1.1.6 Sixth tier of activities **165**
4.2.1.1.7 Seventh tier of activities 171
4.2.1.1.8 Domain wise effect of intervention for first participant 172
4.2.1.2 Participant no.2 - Sam.. 182
4.2.1.2.1 First tier of activities.. 182
4.2.1.2.2 Second tier of activities 184
4.2.1.2.3 Third tier of activities 186
4.2.1.2.4 Fourth tier of activities 187
4.2.1.2.5 Fifth tier of activities 189
4.2.1.2.6 Domain wise effect of intervention for second participant 190
4.2.2 Pre post test score comparison of Sensory profile 196
4.2.2.1 Participant no 1 -Aman... 197

    4.2.2.2 Participant no.3 -John 198

    4.2.2.3 Participant no.2 - Sam...200

    4.2.2.4 Participant no.4 - Roshan...203

5. SUMMARY, FINDINGS AND SUGGESTIONS 208

5.1 Study in Retrospect..209

  5.1.1 Restatement of the problem..209

  5.1.2 Variables of the study 209

  5.1.3 The research question and hypotheses 209

  5.1.4 Method...210

    5.1.4.1 Sample for the study 210

    5.1.4.2 Tools used for the study...211

    5.1.4.3 Research Design..211

    5.1.4.4 Procedure...212

    5.1.4.5 Analysis of data...213

5.2 Major Findings 213

5.3 Tenability of Hypotheses 216

5.4 Implications of the study.. 218

5.5 Limitations of the Study 219

5.6 Suggestions for Further Research 221

References... 224

Appendix.. 247

1. INTRODUCTION

1.1 An overview of Autism

1.2 Statement of the problem

1.3 Variables of the study

1.4 Hypotheses

1.5 Method

1.6 Outline of the thesis

After long years of being regarded as a mental illness or emotional maladjustment, autism is now regarded as a biological disorder that is due to organic rather than psychological causes. More specifically, autism is a neurological or brain based developmental disorder that particularly manifests as problems in cognition, communication and interaction. In the past 30 years, the prevalence rate of autism has skyrocketed, and it continues to rise. For the child with autism and his or her family, the disorder is a lifelong challenge. The onset typically occurs before three years of age (Marohn, 2002). Whatever the diagnosis, appropriate education and treatment based on the child's abilities and needs can help children develop to their full potential. All too often children with autism are viewed as members of a group, with little interest or concern shown towards each child as an individual. This is clearly not the intent of the present study. The goal here is to strengthen the perceptions towards the unique qualities of each child.

1.1 An overview of Autism

"If you've met one person with autism, you've met one person with autism." - Dr.Stephen Shore

Arrays of problems are relatively common among autistic people such as seizure disorders, gastrointestinal issues, mental retardation and mental illness. Many autistic people have no apparent mental or physical illness at all. A majority of autistic people are either hyper or hypo sensitive to light, sound, crowds and other external stimulation. Some have both hyper and hypo sensitivities. This often results in autistic people covering their ears, avoiding or reacting negatively to brightly lit areas, or -- on the other hand -- crashing hard into sofas and craving strong bear hugs. While it is unusual to find an autistic person who is obviously physically disabled because of the disorder, most autistic people do have some level of fine and gross motor difficulty.

Teaching children with autism is a challenging endeavor for educators and parents. The children present a unique array of problems that are perplexing because they often seem inconsistent with what is understood about human learning and behavior. It is generally assumed in education that all children follow a similar developmental path, albeit at various rates. Yet children with autism display peculiar styles of social, communicative and interpersonal relationships that seem to follow a different path. An understanding of these developmental differences must be incorporated into intervention in order to embrace the children's social perspective fully, and to develop and use strategies that promote communication and socialization and to assist children with autism through the maze of interpersonal relationships.

There are many shades of autism depending on which behavior is predominant and how severe it is. Autistic Spectrum Disorder (ASD) has been proposed as an umbrella term to include the whole range of autistic symptoms from mild to severe (Wing, 1997; Rapin, 2002). This term reflects the unifying social deficit more poignantly than the term 'pervasive developmental disorders,' and it mirrors the clinically common scenario of a case that does not meet the DSM-IV/ICD-10 criteria strictly but have significant impairments in social skills, pragmatic communication, or sensorimotor behavior.

1.1.1 Epidemiology

Epidemiology is a tool that is useful for describing the occurrence of and risk factors for a disease or condition in human populations. The measure of disease occurrence in a population is based on two parameters: Prevalence and Incidence. Prevalence is typically described as a snapshot of the extent of disease in a population. On the other hand, incidence reflects the number of newly occurring cases. The most commonly used measure of disease frequency for most developmental disabilities, including autism, is prevalence, which has been used to approximate incidence because measurement of the true incidence of autism is problematic. Parents usually become concerned by 18 months of age, but do not present to the primary care provider with these concerns until 6 months later and considerable time lapses between first parental concern and the final definitive diagnosis (Wiggins, Baio & Rice, 2006). In the current state of knowledge, failure to diagnose ASD earlier is unacceptable.

Since the 1960s, with the conduct of the first prevalence studies of autism, a solid body of literature examining the prevalence of autism from population-based studies has been accumulating. Recent estimates have placed the prevalence of autism in the U.S. at approximately 1 in 88 people (CDC, 2012). At India's current population, this means there are more than 2 million autistic persons in the country. This estimate assumes that there are no significant variations in this rate worldwide, which is a question that has not yet been addressed by epidemiologists outside the West. While the disorder is not rare, the majority of autistic people in India has not been diagnosed and do not receive the services they need. This problem occurs in many countries, but is especially true in India where there is a tremendous lack of awareness and misunderstanding about autism among the medical professionals, who may either misdiagnose or under diagnose the condition.

As per the studies conducted by the Child Developmental Centre, Trivandrum, Kerala, the current epidemiologic estimates are approximately 1.7 million individuals with autism in India (Nair, 2006). ASDs occur in all racial, ethnic, and socioeconomic groups, but are four times more likely to occur in boys than in girls.

Autism is predominantly a male condition. If one takes the population of autism as a whole (75% of whom not only have autism but also have mental handicap), the sex ratio is 4:1 (male: female) (Rutter, 1978). If one takes just the 'pure' cases of autism (who are also sometimes referred to as having Asperger Syndrome), whose IQs are in the normal range, the sex ratio is even more dramatic: 9:1 (male: female) (Wing & Gould, 1979). Without doubt, then, autism (and Asperger Syndrome) has a strong relationship with being male.

The number of reported cases of autism increased dramatically in the 1990s and early 2000s. This increase is largely attributable to changes in diagnostic practices, referral patterns, availability of services, age at diagnosis, and public awareness, (Rutter, 2005, Newschaffer et al., 2007) though unidentified environmental risk factors cannot be ruled out.

1.1.2 Characteristics and Diagnosis

Basic characteristics that define autism include the following: difficulty developing relationships with people; delayed speech acquisition and inability to use speech once it develops; repetitive and stereotypical behaviors; lack of imagination; good rote memory; obsessive insistence on sameness of routine; normal physical appearance (Turnbull, Turnbull, Shank & Leal, 1995).

Various stereotypical behaviors are commonly seen among people with autism. Some of the most known are 'body-rocking', hand/limb 'flapping', 'head-banging' and 'spinning'. These might be engaged in at various times: when agitated, when aroused or active, when happy, when excited, when angry and even when simply comfortable and relaxed. These behaviors can be simply automatic, they can be learned and copied, they can be exaggerations of sporadic habits, which nearly everyone has (foot tapping for example), and mostly they express or produce a stimulating feeling or sensation.

Rhythmical motions are good ways of imposing order and control on one's self and the environment and this order is something most people with autism seem to both desire and need. There is a common incidence of interest in spinning around and in watching spinning objects, the dizziness spinning evoke may be enjoyable, as may be the elimination of other information.

ICD-10 Criteria for "Childhood Autism"(F84.0) (20)

A. Abnormal or impaired development is evident before the age of 3 years in at least one of the following areas:

1. Receptive or expressive language as used in social communication;
2. The development of selective social attachments or of reciprocal social interaction;
3. Functional or symbolic play.

B. A total of at least six symptoms from (1), (2) and (3) must be present, with at least two from (1) and at least one from each of (2) and (3)

1. Qualitative impairment in social interaction is manifest in at least two of the following areas:

    a. Failure adequately to use eye-to-eye gaze, facial expression, body postures, and gestures to regulate social interaction;

    b. Failure to develop (in a manner appropriate to mental age, and despite ample opportunities) peer relationships that involve a mutual sharing of interests, activities and emotions;

- c. Lack of socio-emotional reciprocity as shown by an impaired or deviant response to other people's emotions; or lack of modulation of behavior according to social context; or a weak integration of social, emotional, and communicative behaviors;
- d. Lack of spontaneous seeking to share enjoyment, interests, or achievements with other people (e.g. a lack of showing, bringing, or pointing out to other people objects of interest to the individual).

2. Qualitative abnormalities in communication as manifest in at least one of the following areas:
   - a. Delay in or total lack of, development of spoken language that is not accompanied by an attempt to compensate through the use of gestures or mime as an alternative mode of communication (often preceded by a lack of communicative babbling);
   - b. Relative failure to initiate or sustain conversational interchange (at whatever level of language skills are present), in which there is reciprocal responsiveness to the communications of the other person;
   - c. Stereotyped and repetitive use of language or idiosyncratic use of words or phrases;
   - d. Lack of varied spontaneous make-believe play or (when young) social imitative play

3. Restricted, repetitive, and stereotyped patterns of behavior, interests, and activities are manifested in at least one of the following:
   - a. An encompassing preoccupation with one or more stereotyped and restricted patterns of interest that are abnormal in content or focus; or one or more interests that are abnormal in their intensity and circumscribed nature though not in their content or focus;
   - b. Apparently compulsive adherence to specific, nonfunctional routines or rituals;

    c. Stereotyped and repetitive motor mannerisms that involve either hand or finger flapping or twisting or complex whole body movements;

    d. Preoccupations with part-objects of non-functional elements of play materials (such as their order, the feel of their surface, or the noise or vibration they generate).

C. The clinical picture is not attributable to the other varieties of pervasive developmental disorders; specific development disorder of receptive language (F80.2) with secondary socio-emotional problems, reactive attachment disorder (F94.1) or disinhibited attachment disorder (F94.2); mental retardation (F70-F72) with some associated emotional or behavioral disorders; schizophrenia (F20.-) of unusually early onset; and Rett's Syndrome (F84.12) (World Health Organization, 2007).

Even though a criterion has been set for a diagnosis of autism, autism is a multidimensional disorder. Characteristics vary greatly from one person to another (DPI, 2005 as cited in Gardener, 2009). Where these behaviors are a problem (for example self-injurious behavior'), the reason for their presence must be carefully considered.

1.1.3 Etiological perspective

About 80–85% of cases of autism are idiopathic (without an identifiable risk factor) and 15–20% are secondary (with an identifiable risk factor) (De Long, 1999). Although many causes of autism have been proposed for the idiopathic group, few meet the essential criteria of causation. In order to be causal, an association should be strong, consistent, sufficient, and necessary, and should precede the condition. There should be a close relationship between the cause and the condition, a plausible and coherent biological explanation, and an experimental model. No single factor meets all these criteria. Most likely, it is a heterogeneous disorder caused either by many factors that work independently, or in concert to cause neurological dysfunction, that, in turn, manifests as the syndrome of autism. The foremost among these factors is genetic susceptibility (Gupta, 2004). .

Genetic Factors:

About 3–5% of children with autism have a chromosomal anomaly (Ritvo et al., 1990; Weidmer-Mikhail, Sheldon & Ghaziuddin, 1998). No single genetic abnormality has been proven to be a necessary or sufficient cause of autism. It seems that as many as 15–20 loci on different chromosomes may independently or additively play a minor role in increasing susceptibility to a broad autism phenotype consisting of abnormalities in social and communicative behavior.

A 2005 study done by the Duke Center for Human Genetics at Duke University finds some evidence that complex interactions between GABA (gamma aminobutyric acid) receptor genes might be part of the cause of autism (as cited in Ma et al., 2005). One of the functions of the GABA genes is to inhibit the nerve system from firing. The theory is that somehow GABA genes suffer damage of some kind, leading to an overwhelmed sensory system causing the characteristics or symptoms of autism.

Down syndrome and fragile X are the predominant chromosomal disorders among individuals with autistic disorder (Gillberg & Coleman, 1992). Autistic disorder may occur in as many as 7% of individuals with Down syndrome. The likelihood of autistic disorder in children with Down syndrome is increased if there is history of autism or other pervasive developmental disorders in first- or second-degree relatives, infantile spasms, early hypothyroidism and brain injury following heart surgery (Rasmussen, Borjesson, Wentz & Gillberg, 2001). Among the single-gene disorders, tuberous sclerosis and untreated phenylketonuria (PKU) seem to be the most important associations of autism. Autistic spectrum disorder has been reported in approximately 40% of persons with tuberous sclerosis (Gutierrez, Smalley & Tinguay, 1998., Smalley, 1998), an autosomal dominant disorder that occur due to mutation of the tuberous sclerosis complex 1 (TSC1) or TSC2 genes.

The Center for Disease Control and Prevention, Autism Genome Project studied over 100 genes commonly linked to autism. They looked for rare variants–small deletions or additions to the DNA sequences that make up these genes. They found that people with autism had a higher number of these variants than those without the disorder, and that some of these DNA differences were not inherited. That means these DNA changes occurred either in the egg cell, sperm, or in the developing embryo (Gupta, 2004).

Hu et al. (2009) identified chemical changes in DNA taken from cells of identical twins and sibling pairs, in which only one of the twins or siblings was diagnosed with autism. They found that proteins, as predicted by the observed increase in DNA tagging, were reduced in the autistic brain. Their findings suggests that blocking the chemical tagging of these genes may reverse symptoms of the disorder and demonstrated the feasibility of using more easily accessible cells from blood (or other non-brain tissues) for diagnostic screening.

Prenatal factors:

The risk of autism is associated with several prenatal risk factors. A child's risk of developing autism is associated with the **age of its mother and father** at birth; the biological reasons for this are unknown: possible explanations include increased risk of pregnancy complications; maternal auto immunity, increased risk of chromosomal abnormalities or unstable trinucleotide repeats in the egg and imprinted genes, spontaneous mutations and confounding sociocultural factors in the sperm. Since ages of the father and mother are correlated, it is possible that only the mother's age, or only the father's age, or both, contribute to the risk (Gardener, Spiegelman & Buka, 2009).

Prenatal viral infection has been called the principal non-genetic cause of autism. Prenatal exposure to rubella or cytomegalovirus activates the mother's immune response greatly increases the risk for autism (Patterson, 2009). Congenital rubella syndrome is the most convincing environmental cause. Infection-associated immunological events in early pregnancy may affect neural development more than infections in late pregnancy (Zhou, 2012).

The maternal antibody theory hypothesizes that immunoglobulin G (IgG) in a mother's blood can cross the placenta, enter into the fetus's brain, react against fetal brain proteins, and cause autism. (Dalton et al., 2003). The theory is related to the autoimmune disease hypothesis, except it focuses on maternal antibodies rather than the child's. A 2008 study found that these antibodies bind to fetal brain cells, most commonly in mothers of children with regressive autism (Braunschweig et al., 2008). Another study found that rhesus monkeys exposed during gestation to IgG from mothers of children with ASD demonstrated stereotypies, one of the three main symptoms of autism (Martin et al., 2008).

Many studies point towards 'environmental factors' that causes birth defects: teratogens. It is conceived that a teratogen damages the fetal brain directly or makes it vulnerable to injury by another factor. Time of neural tube closure seems critical for the development of autism because cases of thalidomide embryopathy with symptoms of autism were exposed to thalidomide at the time of neural tube closure (Miller, 1993; Stromland, Nordin, Miller, Akerstrom & Gilberg, 1994).

Moore et al. (2000) reported autistic symptoms in 60% of children exposed to anticonvulsants including valproic acid in utero. Other factors that are suspected to be associated with autism are alcohol, coccaine, polychlorinated polyphenyles(PCBs), retinoids and methyl mercury.

Diabetes in the mother during pregnancy is a significant risk factor for autism; a 2009 meta-analysis found that **gestational diabetes** was associated with a twofold increased risk. Although diabetes causes metabolic and hormonal abnormalities and **oxidative stress,** no biological mechanism is known for the association between gestational diabetes and autism risk (Gardener, Spiegelman & Buka, 2009).

Thyroid problems that lead to thyroxin deficiency in the mother in weeks 8–12 of pregnancy has been postulated to produce changes in the fetal brain leading to autism. Thyroxin deficiencies can be caused by inadequate iodine in the diet, and by environmental agents that interfere with iodine uptake or act against thyroid hormones. Possible environmental agents include flavonoids in food, tobacco smoke, and most herbicides. This hypothesis has not been tested (Roman, 2007). A related untested hypothesis is that exposure to pesticides could combine with suboptimal iodine nutrition in a pregnant mother and lead to autism in the child.

Exposure to life events or environmental factors that distress an expectant mother, has been hypothesized to contribute to autism, possibly as part of a gene-environment interaction. Autism has been reported to be associated with prenatal stress both with retrospective studies that examined stressors such as job loss and family discord, and with natural experiments involving prenatal exposure to storms; animal studies have reported that prenatal stress can disrupt brain development and produce behaviors resembling symptoms of autism (Kinney, Munir, Crowley & Miller, 2008).

Perinatal Factors:

Perinatal and obstetric factors have not emerged as important in the etiology of autism. Higher incidence of second- or third-trimester uterine bleeding and prolonged labor has been reported in several studies (Juul-Dam, Townsend & Courchesne, 2001). Other complications that have been reported inconsistently include induction of labor, prolonged and precipitous labor, and oxygen requirement at birth.

A 2007 review of risk factors found associated obstetric conditions that included low birth weight and gestation duration, and hypoxia during childbirth. This association does not demonstrate a causal relationship; an underlying cause could explain both autism and these associated conditions (Kolevzon, Gross & Reichenberg, 2007).

Postnatal Factors:

A wide variety of postnatal contributors to autism have been proposed, including gastrointestinal or immune system abnormalities, allergies, and exposure of children to drugs, vaccines, infection, certain foods, or heavy metals.

It is unclear if immune dysfunction is the cause or effect of autism or whether it is primary or secondary to a genetic abnormality or an infection). A viral infection in utero can damage the developing immune system of the fetus. Congenital rubella infection is associated with immune dysfunction, autoimmune diseases, and autism. Other prenatal infections, such as rubella, cytomegalovirus, herpes simplex, syphilis, and toxoplasmosis, have been implicated in the causation of autism. Infections can alter antigenic determinants on cell surface, activate immune cells, and influence the nervous system through cytokine release. Over 60 different microbial peptides have been reported to cross-react with human brain tissue and myelin basic protein and are potentially capable of triggering autoimmune encephalomyelitis Moreover, the neuronal injury in autism is postulated to occur so early during gestation, at or before 5-6 weeks of pregnancy, that immunological dysfunction is unlikely to be the primary cause of autism (Gupta, 2004).

The saga of measles, mumps, and rubella (MMR) vaccination and autism started when Wakefield et al. reported a series of 12 cases that allegedly developed regressive autism after receiving MMR vaccination. The symptoms were apparently mediated by MMR vaccine-induced enterocolitis that, in turn, allowed neurotoxic metabolites to be absorbed from the gut (Cook,1990; Fatemi, Halt, Stary, Kanodia, Schulz & Realmuto, 2002). However, population-based studies of autism have not found any association between autism and MMR vaccination (Taylor et al, 1999; Madsen et al., 2002).

Many parents of autistic children report having given prolonged courses of antibiotic drugs for infections by about one and a half years before the diagnosis of the disorder. Broad-spectrum antibiotics kill good as well as bad bacteria in the gut leading to weakness in the intestinal membrane. Large molecules of substances that should not be absorbed are hence taken in. The condition is called Leaky Gut Syndrome. Although a few clinic-based studies have shown increased prevalence of GI (Gastro Intestinal) symptoms in children with autism, population-based studies have failed to show an association of GI disorders, including Irritable Bowel, with autism.

The main premise of the "gut" theory of autism is that the gastrointestinal(GI) tract is unable to adequately metabolize opioids derived from dietary sources, in particular foods that contain gluten and casein, and permits them to be absorbed via an abnormally permeable intestinal membrane (D'Eufemia, et al., 1996, Horvath, Papadimitriou, Rabsztyn, Drachenberg & Tildon, 1999). These peptides cross the blood-brain barrier and bind to the opioid receptors producing symptoms of autism, such as inattention, inability to learn, and poor social interaction. Children with autism have been reported to have increased urinary excretion of low-molecular-weight peptides and increased opioid levels in cerebrospinal fluid. The gastrointestinal symptoms, such as bulky, malodorous, loose stools or intermittent diarrhea, in children with autistic spectrum disorder result in such cases (Reichelt, Knivsberg, Lind & Nodland, 1991). The now largely discounted association between MMR vaccination and autism was allegedly mediated by vaccine-induced enterocolitis resulting in absorption of toxic peptides (Wakefield, Murch & Anthony, 1998).

1.1.4 Neurological basis of autism

Brain is the final pathway to which all the etiological factors discussed above lead. There is sufficient evidence in the neuroscience literature that autistic symptoms occur because of functional or structural abnormalities of the brain. Epilepsy has been reported in as many as 4–30% of children with autism and pervasive developmental disorders, providing additional support for the neurogenic basis of autism. Clinical seizures, usually partial, occur more often in infancy and adolescence (Giovanardi, Posar & Parmeggiani, 2000).

The symptoms of autism result from maturation-related changes in various systems of the brain. Its mechanism can be divided into two areas: the pathophysiology of brain structures and processes associated with autism, and the neuropsychological linkages between brain structures and behaviors. The behaviors appear to have multiple pathophysiologies (Penn, 2006).

Neuroanatomical studies and the associations with teratogens strongly suggest that autism's mechanism includes alteration of brain development soon after conception (Arndt, Stodgell & Rodier, 2005). This anomaly appears to start a cascade of pathological events in the brain that are significantly influenced by environmental factors.

Just after birth, the brain of autistic children tend to grow faster than usual, followed by normal or relatively slower growth in childhood. It is not known whether early overgrowth occurs in all autistic children. It seems to be most prominent in brain areas underlying the development of higher cognitive specialization. (Geschwind, 2009). About 15–30% of children with autism have macrocephaly, due to larger brain volume in autism (Piven, Arndt, Bailey & Andreasen, 1996). While autistic individuals continue to have a larger head circumference throughout their life, their brain volume decreases after increasing for a few years after birth (suggesting a neuropathological process that begins before birth but continues postnatally).

Numerous studies have focused on the cortical and sub cortical systems related to language and cognitive processes, that is, on areas of the frontal and temporal lobes as well as the neo striatum, sensory processing systems and cerebellum. Neuro pathological studies have suggested cellular changes in the hippocampus and amygdala.

The cerebellum plays an important role in language, emotion, and motor-attentional systems through its connections with frontal lobe, thalamus and other areas of the brain. It is plausible that abnormalities of the cerebellum or a disruption of its neural networks with the other areas of the brain contributes to symptoms pertaining to these domains. Several neuropathological studies have found low Purkinje and granular cell count in the cerebellar hemispheres of individuals with autism (Bailey et al., 1998).

The limbic system is believed to be the socio-emotional brain, and is, thus, a plausible candidate for the source of social symptoms in autism (Brothers, 1990).

Animal lesion studies, single cell recording studies and neurological studies (Brothers, Ring & Kling, 1990) suggested that social intelligence was a function of three regions: the amygdala, the orbito-frontal cortex (OFC), and the superior temporal sulcus and gyrus (STG). The theory proposes that the amygdala is one of the several neural regions that are necessarily abnormal in autism.

Citing a functional MRI (fMRI) study in which patients with autism or Asperger's syndrome did not activate their amygdala when judging what that other person might be thinking or feeling by looking at his face, Baron-Cohen et al. proposed an "amygdale theory of autism" (Baron-Cohen, Ring, Bullmore, Wheelwright, Ashwin & Williams, 2000). Howard et al., (2000) showed that people with high-functioning autism have a neuropsychological profile characteristic of amygdala damage, in particular impairment in recognizing faces and facial expressions. Using quantitative magnetic resonance (MR) images analysis techniques, they demonstrated bilateral enlargement of the amygdala in these individuals.

Association between autism and Mo¨bius sequence suggests that brainstem may be involved in a few cases of autism (Gillberg, & Steffenburg, 1989). Mo¨bius sequence is characterized by hypoplasia of cranial nerve nuclei resulting in congenital palsy of the sixth and seventh cranial nerves. The lesions in brainstem at an early stage of embryogenesis perhaps damage the cerebral-cerebellar connections that are necessary for the development of higher cognitive functions (Skoyles, 2002). Such brainstem-cerebellar dysfunction was suggested by the finding of abnormal oculomotor movements and brainstem potentials in children with autism (Rosenhall, Johansson & Gillberg, 1988).

Ornitz et al. found abnormal responses to vestibular stimulation in autistic children (1985). Therefore, it is plausible that brainstem dysfunction can cause some symptoms of autism such as transitioning from one activity to another, vestibular dysfunction, and abnormal sensory processing.

Basal ganglia include caudate nucleus, putamen, globus pallidus, nucleus accumbens, and substantia nigra. An increase in the volume of the caudate nuclei, proportional to the increased total brain volume, was found to be associated with compulsions and rituals, complex motor mannerisms, and resistance to change in autism in an MRI study of the brain (Sears, Vest, Mohamed, Bailey, Ranson & Piven, 1999).

Cognitive and communication deficits in autism make cerebral cortex a plausible "home for autism."Prefrontal dysfunction is suggested by abnormalities in voluntary suppression of oculomotor responses to visual targets. Delayed metabolic maturation of frontal lobes causing functional deficits in object permanence and theory of mind has been reported (Minshew, Luna & Sweeney, 1999).

As the symptoms of autism originate in multiple areas of the brain, abnormal chemical neurotransmission among these areas may be the root cause of autism. There is some evidence to support the neurochemical basis of autism, but like neuroimaging, neurochemical findings in autism are inconsistent and contradictory.

Serotonin is involved in perception and sensory filtration of stimuli and in social attachment (Chamberlain & Herman, 1990) and its dysfunction can plausibly cause autistic symptoms; the exact nature of serotonergic dysfunction in autism is still unknown despite a litany of studies.

Improvement in behavioral symptoms of autism by haloperidol, a dopamine antagonist, suggests that dopaminergic systems are involved in autism. Risperidone, an atypical neuroleptic and a potent antagonist of the postsynaptic dopamine D2 receptor, is effective in controlling some symptoms of autism, such as tantrums, aggression, and self-injurious behavior (Cohen, Caparulo, Shaywitz & Bowers, 1977). Higher levels of homovanillic acid, a metabolite of dopamine, have been reported in low functioning autistic children. The dopaminergic system influences selective attention and motor behavior. Dysfunction of dopaminergic transmission in the prefrontal cortex may cause symptoms of inattention and hyperactivity in autism, while in the basal ganglia it may cause motor stereotypies (Young, Kavanagh, Anderson, Shaywitz & Cohen, 1982). The role of dopamine in autism is, however, inconclusive, because drugs that antagonize dopamine, such as risperidone, as well as those that enhance its transmission, such as methylphenidate, are helpful in children with autism.

Opioid overactivity in the brain has been proposed to be the cause of poor socialization, decreased sensitivity to pain, and self-injurious behavior in autism (Gillberg, Terenius & Lonnerholm, 1985). The limbic system, which is implicated in the causation of socio-emotional problems of autism, is rich in endogenous opioid receptors. An unsubstantiated theory about the role of exogenous opioids in autism is in vogue in the alternative medicine camp. According to this theory, an excess of opioids enter the bloodstream from the gut through a defective mucosal barrier. Opioids are produced in the gut from incompletely digested gluten and/or casein due to the failure of intestinal peptidases to convert opioids to innocuous metabolites (Reichelt, Knivsberg, Lind & Nodland, 1991).

The results of two systematic trials of dietary exclusion of gluten and casein have been equivocal. Dysfunction of other neurotransmitter systems, such as catecholamines, glutamate, gamino butyric acid (GABA), neuropeptides, and nicotine, has been proposed to cause symptoms of autism. Catecholamines are plausible candidates for involvement in autism because noradrenergic cells in the locus ceruleus regulate attention, behavioral flexibility, filtering of irrelevant stimuli, arousal, anxiety, and learning, which are impaired in autistic individuals. Hormones such as oxytocin, insulin-like growth factor, and testosterone have also been suggested to have or affect neurotransmitter function (Insel, O'Brien & Leckman, 1999).

It seems that no single neurotransmitter has a monopoly on the symptoms of autism, but they modulate one another's actions to cause a unique mix of symptoms in each patient. Because of the unique pattern of neurochemical dysfunction in each patient, no single drug works in all the patients.

Thus, evidence is mounting that multiple genes are involved, their expression being influenced through environmental interaction, with the immune system playing a role in many cases. There are likely to be critical periods when the active process of epigenetic changes pushes the neurodevelopmental trajectory toward the autism spectrum.

1.1.5 Management

Autism Spectrum Disorders (ASDs), similar to other neurodevelopmental disabilities, are generally not "curable," and chronic management is required. Although outcomes are variable and specific behavioral characteristics change over time, most children with ASDs remain within the spectrum as adults and, regardless of their intellectual functioning, continue to experience problems with independent living, employment, social relationships, and mental health (Howlin, 2003, as cited in Volkmar, Paul, Klin, & Cohen, 2005). The primary goals of treatment are to minimize the core features and associated deficits, maximize functional independence and quality of life, and alleviate family distress. Facilitating development and learning, promoting socialization, reducing maladaptive behaviors, and educating and supporting families can help accomplish these goals. No single treatment is best, and treatment is typically tailored to the child's needs.

Treatments fall into three major categories: medical management, educational interventions and family support.

1.1.5.1. Medical management:

Optimization of medical care is very likely to have a positive impact on habilitative progress and quality of life. In addition to routine preventive care and treatment of acute illnesses, management of sleep dysfunction, gastro intestinal problems, coexisting challenging behaviors or psychiatric conditions, and associated medical problems, such as seizures, may be particularly important. Medications have not been proven to correct the core deficits of ASDs and are not the primary treatment. However, associated maladaptive behaviors or psychiatric co morbidities may interfere with educational progress, socialization, health or safety, and quality of life. These behaviors may be amenable to psychopharmacologic intervention or, in some cases, treatment of underlying medical conditions that are causing or exacerbating the behaviors is contributory. Effective medical management may allow a child with an ASD to benefit more optimally from educational interventions.

1.1.5.2. Educational Interventions:

A variety of specific methodologies is used in educational programs for children with ASDs. Detailed reviews of intervention strategies to enhance communication, teach social skills, and reduce interfering maladaptive behaviors have been published in recent years. Brief descriptions of selected methodologies are provided below:

Applied Behavior Analysis (ABA): "Applied" means "practice", "Behavior analysis" may be read as "learning theory," Applied Behavior Analysis focuses on the principles that explain how learning takes place. Positive reinforcement is one such principle. When a behavior is followed by some sort of reward, the behavior is more likely to be repeated. Through decades of research, the field of behavior analysis has developed many techniques for increasing useful behaviors and reducing those that may cause harm or interfere with learning. It focuses on what people say and do (behavior), and utilizes experimental analyses of environmental influences on behavior to derive techniques for behavior change. ABA helps us to understand how people access reinforcement for different behaviors and effectively "learn" the behaviors that provide reinforcers. The first to "package" ABA principles as a treatment for individuals with autism was O. Ivar Lovaas. His "UCLA Young Autism Project" (1987) is perhaps the most widely cited treatment study of individuals with autism (as cited in Simpson, 2005).

Functional behavior analysis, or functional assessment, is an important aspect of behaviorally based treatment of unwanted behaviors. FBA is generally directed toward determining an appropriate intervention for specific behavioral issues, rather than toward skill building. The goal is to identify antecedent conditions and the sources of reinforcement that produce and maintain behavior problems. Most problem behaviors serve an adaptive function of some type and are reinforced by their consequences, such as attainment of (1) adult attention, (2) a desired object, activity, or sensation, or (3) escape from an undesired situation or demand. Functional assessment is a rigorous, empirically based method of gathering information that can be used to maximize the effectiveness and efficiency of behavioral support interventions

(O'Neill, et al., 1996). It includes formulating a clear description of the problem behavior (including frequency and intensity); identifying the antecedents, consequences, and other environmental factors that maintain the behavior; developing hypotheses that specify the motivating function of the behavior; and collecting direct observational data to test the hypothesis. Functional analysis also is useful in identifying antecedents and consequences that are associated with increased frequency of desirable behaviors so that they can be used to evoke new adaptive behaviors.

Discrete Trial Training (DTT): Discrete Trial Training (DTT) is a method of teaching in simplified and structured steps. Instead of teaching an entire skill in one go, the skill is broken down and "built-up" using discrete trials that teach each step one at a time (Smith, 2001). A trial is considered as a single teaching unit. A discrete trial follows the basic format of presentation of an instruction or request (called a "discriminative stimulus"), an expected response from the learner, and a consequence delivered by the instructor. If required, a prompt (an additional stimulus that helps the learner to make the correct response) may be administered as well. Discrete trials are defined and scripted to make sure every trial is run the same way. By running each trial the same way, it allows a Behavior Analyst to identify why a trial procedure might not be working and change it. This general format allows for several interpretations of how antecedents, learner responses, and consequents are to be rendered. By breaking down tasks into short manageable trials and using suitable prompts and guidance 'DTT maximises children's success and minimises their failures' (Smith, 2001, p. 87). A significant amount of research supports the use of DTT with children with ASD in a variety of settings. However, caution should be exercised when assuming that DTT should be used in preference to all other interventions for all children with ASD, especially over extensive periods.

Picture Exchange Communication System (PECS): PECS was developed in 1985 by Lori Frost and Andrew Bondy as a unique augmentative/alternative communication intervention package for individuals with autism spectrum disorder and related developmental disabilities. The program is intended to provide nonverbal individuals with a mode of expressive communication. Specifically, line drawings are used to represent everyday objects, foods, and activities, and the PECS protocol begins with building simple requests. The learner delivers the picture representation of the object, food, or activity to the instructor and then receives what is represented in the picture. As the learner becomes more proficient in requesting preferred items, carrier phrases are added, such as "I want candy." The PECS system is grounded in basic behavioral principles such as shaping, differential reinforcement, and transfer of stimulus control. Frost and Bondy (1994) suggest that after students have mastered PECS it may be appropriate to begin introducing a pointing system or a voice output communication device. They recommend that children are not forced to speak. PECS is widely used in preschools. It was created with families, educators, and resident care providers in mind, and so is readily used in a range of settings.

Pivotal Response Training (PRT): PRT was developed by Koegel and Schreibman (1987). The intent of PRT is to apply educational techniques in pivotal areas that affects numerous target behaviors. Pivotal areas when impacted result in substantial collateral gains in other important areas of development. This technique is related to incidental teaching and includes didactic instruction, modeling, role playing, and feedback. The instructor capitalizes on the learner's interests, motivation, and needs, using naturally occurring opportunities as the basis for instruction. The core considerations in PRT are motivation and the ability to respond to multiple cues, both of which are considered "pivotal" behaviors. Motivation is a pivotal behavior because it leads to concomitant changes in other related behaviors (Koegel et al., 1987). Reinforcement is direct, and is specifically related to the behavior being taught. The behaviors most likely to change through this technique are speech and language, social behavior, and disruptive responses . As a more natural (or social-pragmatic) form of intervention, PRT may be more appealing to parents and educators because it does not involve the withholding of reinforcers and the structure or repetition of structured interventions that characterize discrete trials.

Facilitated Communication: Facilitated communication (FC) is an augmentative communication method that purportedly permits persons with communication and other disabilities to demonstrate unanticipated communication that significantly exceeds what is considered to be the limits of their abilities. The technique involves supporting a nonverbal individual's hand to make it easier for him/her to type out words on a typewriter, computer keyboard, or other communication device (Jacobson, Mulick & Schwartz, 1995). Assisted by hand over hand support or other types of physical assistance from an individual without disabilities, these people are able to type extra ordinary FC enhanced thoughts and ideas .After only minimal experience with FC, people with severe disabilities allegedly have communicated that they have normal intelligence and advanced social skills and knowledge. Biklen (1992) states that individuals with Global Apraxia may appear to have typical intelligence and language processing abilities. Thus when permitted to use FC, these persons purportedly reveal normal intelligence and communication abilities; however, because of its interactive connections and lack of scientific support, controversy also followed FC (Calculator 1992; Rimland, 1992; Schopler, 1992).

Structured Teaching : Structured teaching is a visually based approach to creating highly structured environments that support individuals with autism in a variety of educational, community, and home/living settings (Mesibov, Shea & Schopler, 2005). The Treatment and Education of Autistic and Related Communication Handicapped Children (TEACCH) method, developed by Schopler, Mesibov & Hearsey (1995) attempts to build on the child's strengths and interests rather than drilling deficit areas. TEACCH may be categorized as an eclectic program because of its developmental and behavioral underpinnings (Schopler & Mesibov, 1995). It is one of the most frequently replicated models for autism intervention and is especially popular among public school special education programs.

Developmental Models: Since autism is a social disorder, building social relationships is the core of treatment. This is done by providing opportunities for social interaction and play at home, in an integrated preschool, and during one-to-one teaching. The program is geared toward children from ages 2 to 5 years. Curriculum emphasizes building communication, play, sensory, and motor skills, and promotes personal independence and participation in social routines. The Denver Model is a comprehensive "best practices" model without a narrow theoretical underpinning. The Denver model, is based largely on remediating key deficits in imitation, emotion sharing, theory of mind, and social perception by using play, interpersonal relationships, and activities to foster symbolic thought and teach the power of communication (Handleman & Harris, 2001.)

Multi sensory stimulation: Multi sensory stimulation is a therapeutic regime used for people with developmental disabilities, dementia and brain injury. This involves providing sensory stimulation through multiple modalities (tactile, visual, auditory, gustatory, olfactory and proprioceptive) to maximize arousal and awareness in the person. The concept originated in Netherlands in early 1970s by two Dutch therapists Hulsegge and Verheul, (as cited in Fowler,

1997) when it was named as Snoezelan meaning 'to explore' and 'to relax'. Multi sensory environments provide opportunity to enjoy and control a variety of sensory experiences. Recently the use of this intervention has extended throughout the world and can be used in all facets of life. The method conventionally requires a snoezelen room with equipments to deliver stimuli to various senses like using lighting effects, music, sounds, scents etc. Different materials of different textures on the wall and floor can be explored using tactile senses. The approach to using a Multi-Sensory Environment is generally non-directive, without the need for intellectual or verbally mediated activity in terms of following instructions or rules, and regular exposure seems to be more effective. Essentially, one would allow the user of the space the time and opportunity to experience at their own pace what the room has to offer. One may not use or activate immediately all equipment that the room has available, but gradually introduce more of the sensory stimulation, allowing the cues given by the client to guide the career (Fisher, Murray & Bundy, 1991; Ping, 2013).

1.1.5.3 Family support:

Management should focus not only on the child but also on the family. Although parents once were viewed erroneously as the cause of a child's ASD, it is now recognized that parents play a key role in effective treatment. Having a child with an ASD has a substantial effect on a family. Parents and siblings of children with ASDs experience more stress and depression than those of children who are typically developing or even those who have other disabilities (Gray, 2002) Supporting the family and ensuring its emotional and physical health is an extremely important aspect of overall management of ASDs.

Physicians and other health care professionals can provide support to parents by educating them about ASDs; providing anticipatory guidance; training and involving them as co therapists; assisting them in obtaining access to resources; providing emotional support through traditional strategies such as empathetic listening and talking through problems; and assisting them in advocating for their child's or sibling's needs (Myers, Johnson & Council on children with disabilities, 2007). In some cases, referral of parents for counseling or other appropriate mental health services may be required. The need for support is longitudinal, although the specific needs may vary throughout the family life cycle.

1.2 Statement of the problem

The purpose of this study is to examine the effectiveness of multisensory stimulation procedure in the management of autism.

The central research question is:

- Does the use of multi sensory stimulation procedure prove effective in the management of autism?

The explanation of the key variables is detailed in the following pages.

1.3 Variables of the Study

1.3.1. Multisensory Stimulation

Senses are physiological capacities of organisms that provide data for perception. Human beings have a multitude of senses. The human brain has evolved to learn and operate in natural environments in which behavior is often guided by information integrated across multiple sensory modalities. Multisensory interactions are ubiquitous in the nervous system and occur at early stages of perceptual processing (Shams & Seitz, 2008). Therefore, unisensory-training protocols used for skill acquisition can provide unnatural settings and do not tap into multisensory learning mechanisms that have evolved to produce optimal behavior in the naturally multisensory environment.

On a daily basis, we experience events that simultaneously stimulate more than one sense. We use our multiple senses to take in this varied information, and combine them to give us a clear understanding of the world around us. We learn during childhood how to do this. We gain the ability to use all of our senses together to plan a response to anything we notice in our environment .There is extensive evidence that the stimulation an organism receives from its external environment has a profound effect on its later behavior. Specifically, heightened sensory stimulation and opportunities for problem solving enhance performance on a variety of learning and memory tasks (Renner & Rosenzweig, 1987). Behavioral evidence of human perception and action, indicates that organisms make use of multisensory stimulation. Under normal circumstances, multisensory stimulation leads to enhanced perceptions of, and facilitated responses to, objects in the environment (Barakova & Chonnaparamutt, 2009).

In the present study, multisensory stimulation refers to the therapeutic use of sensory stimulation methods incorporated into daily activities. The researcher introduces various sensory stimulation activities in the behavior modification program to help the child organize information. Multisensory Stimulation is the type, level and combination of sensations that are sufficient to attract an individual's interest (Pagliano, 1999).

Sensory stimulation is used as a way to involve the person with the environment, bring pleasure and it provides a medium for interaction with a person who otherwise, has limited abilities to interact. It has been suggested that positive emotions are associated with situations which present opportunities rather than threats, and with a strategy of approach rather than avoidance (Huppert, 2005 as cited in Forgas, 2006).

Cognitive psychologists suggest that the main ingredient of the intellectual phenomenon is sensory stimulation that allows a human being to apprehend through its senses its environment and respond towards it. Multi Sensory Environments improve the development of thought, intelligence and social skills. This offers people with cognitive impairments and other challenging conditions the opportunity to enjoy and control a variety of sensory experiences. Motivation to be involved in one's daily activities depends largely on the senses. Motivation is the process of arousing action, sustaining the activity in progress and regulating the pattern of activity (Coffer, 1964). Without motivation, an organism would not behave; it would be an inert lump doing virtually nothing. Galvanized into action by a need, it would engage in actions motivated by that need and its actions would continue until the need is satisfied. Behavior is the instrument by which the need is satisfied.

Stimulating the senses can have a positive effect on learning as well as emotional and social growth in a child. Sensory stimulation in learning means having activities that challenge or make use of the five senses. These senses, touch, taste, smell, listening, and visual, must be included in one's learning. Traditional sensory stimulation theory has as its basic premise that effective learning occurs when the senses are stimulated (Laird, 1985). Laird found that the vast majority of knowledge held by adults (75%) is learned through seeing. Hearing is the next most effective (about 13%) and the other senses - touch, smell and taste account for 12% of what we know. By stimulating the senses, especially the visual sense, learning can be enhanced. However, this theory says that if multi-senses are stimulated, greater learning takes place. Stimulation through the senses is achieved through a greater variety of colors, volume levels, strong statements, facts presented visually, use of a variety of techniques and media. We use the information that we get through our senses to remember, understand and form new ideas or solve problems (Laird, 1985).Visual, auditory, kinesthetic (touch and movement-oriented) are the defined areas of sensory learning styles. Learning comes more easily to students when instruction is presented using all three stimuli.

It is challenging to know which sensory activities are best for a child with autism. The goal is to help children achieve an optimal state of alertness so that they are able to attend and learn. Children who seem to lack energy and are "floppy" often benefit from sensory activities that increase alertness. Some autistic children are bouncing off the walls, however, and need sensory activities that help slow them down in order to focus (Smith, 2012).

Children with autism often have impaired abilities to interpret what they see, hear, feel and how their bodies are moving in space. Their brains are unable to organize sensory information when they interact with objects. As a result, they may appear clumsy, find touch aversive, fear movement and be easily overwhelmed. Multisensory stimulation could reduce the distractibility of students and calm them down. It builds trust and positive relationship between therapist and child. It is then they are more able to engage. It heightens their interest and attention and more is the motivational effect (Smith, 2012).

'Communication' is defined by Oxford dictionaries as the imparting or exchanging of information by speaking, writing or by using some other medium. Multi sensory stimulation is this some other medium. However, it is not just some other medium; it is the first and the most basic medium through which information is shared. It is the precursor to speech and language and all higher forms of communication. The beauty of multisensory stimulation is that it can be used to communicate even at the most basic levels, for example, at the mere detection and recognition levels. Using scaffolding it can help a person develop higher order skills such as differentiating between sense experiences. Successful scaffolding depends on the guiding practitioner (Pagliano, 2012).

According to Canadian communication theorist McLuhan (1964), too much attention is placed on the content of the communication and not enough consideration is given to the medium of communications (cited in, Pagliano, 2012). Over time, the association between the medium and message gets so interdependent that the medium influences the way the message is understood. A key part of this message is that social interaction (particularly in the developmental period) through a caring facilitator is essential for neuroplasticity to occur (Lin Lu et al. 2003 as in Pagliano, 2012).

1.3.2 Dependent Variables

In the present study "Management of Autism," from the perspective of a therapist means dealing an autistic person without much difficulty and helping him to develop. The intervention targets improvement of: Motor skills, including fine and gross motor skills, Communication-including social interaction and language of the child, Cognitive skills to improve on imaginative play and develop learning skills The dependent variables were selected for their social significance.

1.3.2.1. Motor skills   A motor skill is any bodily movements that requires the recruitment of both cognitive and physical processes in order to consistently and efficiently accomplish some desired task. Motor skills are typically divided into two categories: gross motor skills and fine motor skills (Wang, 2004) Gross motor skills are those that require the larger muscle groups for function: running, jumping, hopping, climbing and ball skills etc.

Movement disturbance symptoms in individuals with autism have long been not considered an important symptom. During the last decade, Leary & Hill (1996) have offered a radical perspective on this subject. After a thorough analysis of the bibliography on movement impairments in autism, they outlined how deficits in movement preparation and execution could lead to many of the behaviors exhibited by individuals with autism. Difficulties in planning and executing simple discrete movements can lead to problems in learning to coordinate diverse muscle groups into a unitary movement pattern. Moreover, when a person is unable to respond to another's action in a timely fashion, they will miss the positive reinforcement associated with interpersonal interaction (Barakova & Chonnaparamutt, 2009).

Children with autism frequently show developmental delays in developing fine motor skills (Reynolds & Dombeck, 2006). While some children enjoy fine motor activities like lacing their shoes or coloring, others become very agitated when directed to complete fine motor activities. Part of the issue children with autism have with fine motor activities is that they tend to interfere with their need to engage in stereotyped repetitive movements and self-stimulatory behaviors.

As a child develops gross motor skills, other skill areas are also developing, such as eye-hand/foot coordination, sensory functioning (visual, tactile, kinesthetic, auditory modalities), the skills to work and play within a team and sporting environment, and the development of self-confidence and a positive self image (Brereton & Broadbent, 2007). Gross motor difficulties in a child with autism may be in part due to: - proprioception problems (awareness of body in space), lack of motivation to participate in and therefore practice these activities, avoidance because of the social nature of many of these activities (e.g. sports), limited strength or muscle endurance, lack of confidence or a fear of moving equipment and difficulty in problem solving in order to develop skills. Helping kids with autism develop motor skills involves adapting the environment and activities to address sensory motor and learning needs.

1.3.2.2. Communicative skills

One of the most significant goals for an autistic child's individual program plan is to foster increased communication.

Understanding and using nonverbal, as well as verbal, communication is a necessary part of effective information exchange. A timely gesture or facial expression may more clearly express what a person is thinking than the spoken word. Objects, pictures, or written words can also be used in a variety of ways to convey messages. Since individuals on the autism spectrum vary greatly in their communication, and what works for one may not work with the next, we need to have a wide array of tools as we work with each child to build a bridge to effective communication. Not every child with an autism spectrum disorder will have a language problem (Crissey, 2011).

A child's ability to communicate will vary, depending upon his or her intellectual and social development. Some children with autism may be unable to speak. Others may have rich vocabularies and be able to talk about specific subjects in detail. Most children with autism have little or no problem pronouncing words. The majority, however, have difficulty using language effectively, especially when they talk to other people. Many have problems with the meaning and rhythm of words and sentences (National Institute on Deafness and Other Communication Disorders, 2012). They also may be unable to understand body language and the nuances of vocal tones.

1.3.2.3. Cognitive skills

Human cognition involves the perception, processing, acquisition, retrieval, transformation, use and exchange of knowledge. The significant biological impact and serious neurological symptoms of Autism are then clearly expressed in how people with Autism characteristically think and behave. Visual and verbal communication capacities have been shown to affect 90% of learning (and therefore teaching), and underlie most of the complex and higher information processing and memory functions of the brain (Sheinkopff, 2005).

Executive functions (EF) are a broad class of cognitive abilities involved in the regulation of thought and action. This class of higher cognitive abilities supports such functions as strategic planning, impulse control, working memory, organization of mean end behaviors, and flexibility in thought and action. The frontal lobes are heavily involved in these processes. Deficits in EF are well replicated in children with autistic disorder. However, research indicates that autism is related to a specific pattern of deficits in executive skills; i.e., deficits in planning efficiency and preservative responses that indicate difficulties in shifting response set (Smith, 1999).

1.4 Hypotheses

The following research hypotheses are formulated:

1. There is significant difference between the scores assigned by the researcher and the observer for the performance of the first participant in the behavior modification program focusing on multisensory stimulation procedure.

2. There is significant difference between the scores assigned by the researcher and the observer for the performance of the second participant in the behavior modification program focusing on multisensory stimulation procedure.

3. The level of the target behavior of the first participant varies across baseline and treatment phases of the research design when using a multi sensory stimulation procedure.

4. The level of the target behavior of the second participant varies across baseline and treatment phases of the research design when using a multi sensory stimulation procedure.

5. The target behaviors of the first participant show trends during baseline and treatment phases of the research design when using a multi sensory stimulation procedure.

6. The target behaviors of the second participant show trends during baseline and treatment phases of the research design when using a multi sensory stimulation procedure.

7. There will be substantial difference in the Sensory profile of the experimental group, after multi sensory stimulation procedure when compared against the control group.

1.5 Method

The methodology used for the study is briefly described as follows:

1.5.1 Participants

Through a single subject research design with multiple baseline across behaviors, the researcher intends to examine the effectiveness of the multisensory stimulation procedure in the management of motor, communicative and cognitive behavior of children with autism. The participants (N = 4), consists of children with autism drawn purposively from nine clients who fulfilled the inclusion/ exclusion criteria and whose willingness for participation in the study was secured through parental consent. Out of the four, two children, one moderately autistic and the other severely autistic, are chosen for the intervention program. A control group of matched pairs is also selected for pre post temporal comparison of sensory profile variation. The target variables are assessed by examining the progress made by the subject in the activities charted in the intervention program. The dependent variables are observed and measured repeatedly. The performance is compared across conditions- baseline, and intervention phases. The findings of the researcher were checked against the assessments made by a trained observer for the reliability of the procedure.

1.5.2 Tools used for measurement

The following four tools were used by the investigator for the purpose of the study.

1. **Vineland's Social Maturity Scale** (Malin,1992). VSMS gives an index of the child's social and adaptive development and yields a Social Quotient.

2. **Childhood Autism Rating Scale** (Schopler, Reichler, & Renner, 1999). distinguishes children with autism in the mild/moderate/severe range. (CARS)

3. **The Sensory Integration Inventory** (Reisman & Hanschu, 1992) The Sensory Integration Inventory-Revised(SII-R) is used to screen and rule out serious maladaptive behaviors that are not due to sensory dysfunction. For the comparison of profiles, the scores are entered as percentage of sensitivity in each area.

4. **Curriculum Guide for Autistic Children** (Maurice,1996) The module provides a chronological pattern of activities that could be introduced and worked out on children with developmental disabilities. Those activities that the child could not perform were chosen as the tasks to be intervened.

Besides, data about the history and current functional status of the subjects were collected by the researcher with assistance from the special educator, psychologist, speech pathologist and occupational therapist.

1.5.3 Procedure

The four children selected for the study were matched and paired based on age, date of admission to the school (duration of special care), severity of Autism Rating, and Sensory Sensitivity/ Sensory preferences, assessed using the tools mentioned above. An intervention plan with activities tailored according to their subjective needs was prepared for the two participants (experimental group). Three activities requiring motor, communicative and cognitive functioning were chosen and presented to the subject in a session.

The multiple baseline design across behaviors design begins with the concurrent measurements of two or more behaviors of the single participant. After steady state responding has been obtained under baseline conditions, the investigator applied the independent variable to one of the behaviors while maintaining baseline conditions for the other behavior(s). The multisensory stimulation view was held in choosing the activities, the way the activity was executed and providing the consequence. Over and above the research objectives, the ultimate goal was that no attempt at communication should go unnoticed by the child.

A trained psychologist also participated in the study who assessed and scored the experimental subjects during the baseline and intervention phases. An Inter observer agreement was also checked for the reliability of the scoring given to the performance of the children. Posttest scores of the four subjects were done using the Sensory Index inventory after three months. The results were plotted on graphs and visually analyzed.

1.5.4 Analysis of Data

1. *Wilcoxon signed rank test* was done to test whether the scores of the two experimenters varied significantly for the two subjects intervened.

2. *Visual analysis* of the line graphs were plotted for the multiple baseline design and histograms were erected for showing the sensory profile of the four participants.

3. *Effect size calculation* using NAP (Non-overlap of all pairs) method.

1.6 Outline of the thesis

This first chapter gives an overview of autism, states the problem at hand, introduces the variables studied, the research question and hypotheses formed for the study, and finally an outline of the entire study. The wealth of source materials examined and those that have made theoretical and methodological contributions to this project are analyzed in chapter two of this thesis. Chapter three examines in detail the research design, the history and functional status of the participants, the tools used for assessment, the data collection as well as scoring methods used and a session wise narrative of the intervention made. The chapter ends with a note about the statistical techniques employed for analyzing the data. The fourth chapter analyses and discusses the variation in performance noticed in the participants based on the data. The fifth chapter of this thesis draws together the data examined and the resultant findings and suggests ways in which this research can be continued in future to build even further upon our understanding of autism.

2. LITERATURE REVIEW

A detailed analysis of existing research relevant to the topic was conducted. The researcher then attempted to synthesize and evaluate it according to the guiding concept of the research question.

More than 60 years ago, two very similar descriptions of children displaying severe social deficits and unusual behaviors were published - one in English, one in German, both using the term 'autistic'. Leo Kanner in 1943 in Baltimore, USA, described 11 children with 'early infantile autism' in his seminal paper 'Autistic disturbances of affective contact'. In the same year, October 1943, Hans Asperger, in Vienna, Austria, submitted his thesis on 'Autistic psychopathy in childhood', which was published in 1944, describing four children with 'autistic psychopathy'. Both authors used the term 'autistic' which was coined by Bleuler, a Swiss psychiatrist, who used this label to describe the characteristics of individuals with schizophrenia (Lyons & Fitzgerald, 2007).

The earliest as well as the most current theories of autism are based on the premise that persons with autism process sensory information in a way that is different from others (Brock, Brown & Boucher, 2002). Interventions can be effectively presented, and sensory seeking behaviors decreased, once individual sensory needs have been met (Watling & Dietz, 2007).

Kwok, To & Sung (2003) documented that people have their basic human needs, i.e., to seek sensory stimulation, to make sense of the world, for relaxation and for enjoyment. However, if a person fails to fulfill these needs, as people with Pervasive Developmental Disorder (PDD) for example, attention will be turned inwards, resulting in the development of maladaptive behaviors such as self-injury, self-stimulation and stereotype behaviors. People with PDD are living in a relatively sensory deprived world because of their deficits in intellectual and social functioning. Therefore, multi-sensory environment provides a structured environment to fulfill their needs.

Pagliano (1999) states that Multi-Sensory Stimulation (MSS) is in dynamic equilibrium with its user. Therefore, the user can only determine the definition of the multi-sensory stimulation at that time. It can be defined as anything that provides stimulation to our five senses. Based on human's sensory system, the sensory system receives and transmits environmental stimuli from the peripheral sense receptors to the spinal cord and to the brain. There is neural integration at every level of the pathway, reshaping the transmitting information and help the body plan, organize and execute movement via the muscles (Pagliano, 1999). The sensory feedback from a motor response is used in turn to further enhance the body scheme. As when such receptors are used more, they are easier to be activated. However, for people with PLD (Profound Learning Disability), may have problems in receiving or transmitting information. This will result in impairments in vision, hearing, taste, smell and touching. Therefore, if the child's disability has been accurately assessed, it is possible to use MSS to help the child to understand the environment. Also, according to the somatosensory modality, human body consists of the senses of touch, pain, temperature, proprioception and balance.

The findings of Bahrick & Todd (2012) indicate that learning mechanisms operate optimally under multisensory conditions. It is conjectured that perceptual and cognitive mechanisms have evolved for, and are tuned to, processing multisensory signals. Under such a regime, encoding, storing and retrieving perceptual information is intended by default to operate in a multisensory environment, and unisensory processing is often suboptimal, as it would correspond to an artificial mode of processing that does not use the perceptual machinery to its fullest potential. Intersensory processing entails perception of unified and coordinated information across the senses, including visual, auditory, tactile, and proprioceptive stimulation. Critical skills, such as social orienting and joint attention, which are found to be impaired in autism, also rely on a foundation of intersensory functioning. Therefore, an impairment in intersensory processing skills would typically impact social attention to a greater extent than attention to nonsocial events.

Murphy (2009) contributed to the idea that sensory processing is an area of deficit for individuals with autism, and that sensory integration could be a viable treatment option. A quasi-experimental study was made which endeavored to determine whether or not sensory integration (SI) therapy has an effect on development of motor skills in children with autism. The intervention study included two participants who have a primary diagnosis of autism. The intervention showed an increased ability of participants to complete motor tasks they were previously unable to perform. The study showed a positive relationship between the use of sensory integration therapy and further development of motor skills. Participants' ability to complete motor tasks increased, and their tolerance of sensory stimuli also improved as a result of the intervention. Regarding the perceptions of the professionals, the findings indicated a very positive indication for the use of Sensory Integration therapy for improving motor skills in children with autism.

Stevenson, Mark, and Wallace (2012) laid that the process of integrating information across sensory modalities is highly dependent upon the temporal coincidence of the inputs. Audiovisual information is integrated within a range of temporal offsets, known as the temporal binding window (TBW), which varies between individuals. Three particular findings relating to TBW have led to a novel approach to address sensory integration impairments in children with autism. The first is that autistic children have an atypically wide TBW, as measured through manipulations of audiovisual illusions. Second, an individual's TBW is related to their ability to perceptually fuse audiovisual inputs; the narrower the right TBW, the stronger the McGurk effect (tendency to integrate auditory information and the visual cues). The third finding is that the TBW is plastic. Through perceptual feedback training, it was shown that individual's right TBW can be narrowed. These three findings, led to a study of perceptual feedback training in autistic children who may have the ability to narrow their TBW, with a possible positive impact on their ability to integrate multisensory information, specifically speech.

Successful integration of signals from the various sensory systems is crucial for normal sensory–perceptual functioning, allowing for the perception of coherent objects rather than a disconnected cluster of fragmented features. Several prominent theories of autism suggest that automatic integration is impaired in this population, but there have been few empirical tests of this thesis. Russo et al., (2010) conducted a standard electrophysiological metric of multisensory integration (MSI) to test the integrity of auditory–somatosensory integration in children with autism compared to age- and IQ-matched typically developing (TD) children. Participants watched a silent movie during testing, ignoring concurrent stimulation. Significant differences between neural responses to the multisensory auditory-somatosensory stimulus and the unisensory stimuli (the sum of the responses to the auditory and somatosensory stimuli when presented alone) served as the dependent measure. The data revealed group differences in the integration of auditory and somato sensory information that appeared at around 175 milliseconds, and were characterized by the presence of MSI for the TD but not the autism spectrum disorder (ASD) children. Overall, MSI was less extensive in the ASD group.

Gardner (2009) conducted a research to examine the effects of sensory diet interventions on a child with autism to determine whether the intervention program was successful in decreasing a target behavior of aggressive outbursts using a modified alternating treatment (ABAC) design. Results showed a decrease in aggressive outbursts after the first series of techniques were implemented, but it was not clear whether the decrease was a result of the intervention. Further, the results showed that second series of techniques did not have a positive impact on the behavior, yet extraneous variables may have affected the data.

The research of Kwok et al. (2003), listed out nine functions of the multi-sensory stimulation, which included:

- Relaxation
- Developing self-confidence
- Achieving a sense of self-control
- Encouraging exploration and creative activities
- Establishing rapport with care givers
- Providing leisure and enjoyment
- Promoting choice
- Improving attention span
- Reducing challenging behaviors

There is limited research about the effectiveness of multi sensory stimulation (MSS) for people with Profound Learning Disability. Hogg et al., (2001) commented that most MSS research did not adopt both qualitative and quantitative methods and most of them used descriptive or inferential methods to assess the effectiveness of MSS for people with PLD.

Kaplan et al., (2005) found that MSS had a carryover effect for people with learning disabilities. They found that MSS could reduce the challenging behavior, self-injury behavior and stereotypic behavior of people with moderate/severe intellectual disability, autism and severe challenging behaviors. Compared with other adult activity settings, such as activities of daily living skills training, vocational skills training, MSS also showed its superior in reducing the aggression and self-injury behaviors of adults with mental retardation and mental illness (Singh et al., 2004). Besides, compared with other therapies, as hand massage/aromatherapy, relaxation and active therapy (a bouncy castle), MSS and relaxation had a positive effect on concentration and seemed to be the most enjoyable therapies for participants, whereas hand massage/aromatherapy and active therapy had no or even negative effects on concentration and appeared to be less enjoyable (Lindsay et al., 1997).

Sensory integration dysfunction is commonly defined as the "inability to modulate, discriminate, coordinate or organize sensation adaptively" (DiMatties & Sammons, 2003, p.1).Certain signs of a sensory integration dysfunction include, but are not limited to, hyper-or hyposensitivity to touch, poor coordination, and poor behavioral control (Ramirez, 1998). For example, a child with autism who has sensory dysfunction may not have the same response to touch, taste, and sounds as a typically developing child. Often times, an autistic child may become irritated with the noise of the television in the background and complain that the television is too loud, even though others believe it is at a comfortable volume.

A case study done by Case-Smith and Bryan (1999) explored the effectiveness of sensory integrative treatment on the play and social interaction behaviors of autistic preschoolers. An AB single subject design was used. During three weeks of baseline and 10 weeks of intervention, four five-year-old males and one four-year-old male were videotaped during their free play to measure their social interaction behaviors. During the intervention phase, therapy was facilitated by an experienced and certified sensory integration therapist. One child left at eight weeks due to uncontrollable events. The results found that two of the remaining four boys "displayed significant increases on measures of adult interaction". The authors linked sensory integration with positive behavioral changes for autistic children.

Linderman and Stewart (1999) examined the efficacy of sensory integrative approaches and treatments on the behaviors of children with PDD. These behaviors included: social interaction, functional communication during meal times, approach to new activities, response to holding, and response to movement. A single subject AB design using two preschool-aged males was conducted using direct observation and parent interviews to measure the affects of sensory integration treatment on functional behaviors at home. The results concluded that both subjects showed significant improvements and had increases in the following areas: spontaneous speech, purposeful play, attention to activities and conversation. The frequency of disruptive behaviors, such as aggressiveness, appeared to decrease as well. Even though the researchers could not control extraneous variables, such as other interventions, they attributed the success to the positive effects of sensory integration therapy for children with autism. However, replication of this study is needed for future generalization. Some researchers believe that there is not sufficient evidence to be able to reasonably conclude that SI therapy has ever been an effective treatment for children with learning disabilities, autism, or any other developmental disability (Shaw, 2002).

Self-stimulating stereotypic behaviour (SSB) is a maladaptive behaviour not unique to those with autism, yet it is common across this population. These behaviours may be a result of either sensory overload or sensory restriction (Lovas et al., 1987, as cited in Shapiro, Parush, Green & Roth, 1997). SSB may provide stimulation that cannot be acquired otherwise (Carr, 1997 as cited in Shapiro et al., 1997). Even developmentally typical children would suffer adverse effects in sensory-deprived environments similar to the disjointed sensory perceptions of those with autism (Burns, Cox & Plant, 2000). Reduction of SSB has yet to be accomplished through therapy in mentally retarded children (Mason & Iwata, 1990 as cited in Shapiro et al., 1997). However, Holmes (1993) and Reisman, (1993) have suggested that suppression of SSB can lead to dramatic improvements in the child's appropriate behaviour (as cited in Shapiro et al., 1997).

Before the inception of MSS, three separate factors could be seen as major technological and sociological contributions to the evolution of multi-sensory stimulation (Pagliano, 1999). These three factors were the birth of the discotheque with its focus on visual and aural ambience, the popularization of soft play constructions in early childhood centers and the radical revision of expectation in the provision of services for individuals with disabilities (Pagliano, 1999). Then, the idea of MSS was started in 1966 in America (Chitsey et al., 2002).

Chomicz (2013) analyzed a case study on a single participant having autism and sensory processing abnormalities, and studied the efficacy of sensory stimulation to help a student with autism self-regulate. The research utilized an ABAB design to determine whether three interventions (deep pressure using a gym ball, a large pillow (crash pad) to sit on, jump on, and lay on; and a carpeted barrel for the child to lie on, lay in, and rock or roll in/on) helped the participant self-regulate and led to decreases in two specific sensory-seeking behaviors (rocking and spinning). Behaviors were tracked using formal and informal observations, during two meetings, for 20-minute increments. The overall weekly results fluctuated and offered little consistency. However, findings indicated some positive results. Some of the targeted behaviors decreased during Phase B when the interventions were presented, when compared to the baseline (Phase A). The results indicate a decrease in frequency, which suggested that the interventions have played an active role in reducing the undesired spinning and rocking behaviors, ultimately helping the participant self-regulate.

Overland (2010) observed that children having delay in the motor skills to feeding, may benefit from, a sensory-motor based pre-feeding program could be implemented with carefully selected oral sensory-motor exercises and activities. This will allow the child to develop the motor plans for safe nutritive feedings. Once prerequisite oral motor skills have been acquired, sensory exploration techniques and behavioral reinforcements, if needed and appropriate, can be used effectively to expand the diet and increase food quantity.

Robust perception requires that information from by our five different senses be combined at some central level to produce a single unified percept of the world. Recent theory and evidence from many laboratories suggest that the combination does not occur in a rigid, hard-wired fashion, but follows flexible situation-dependent rules that allow information to be combined with maximal efficiency As Ernst and Bülthoff (2004) pointed out in their review, the key to robust perception is the efficient combination and integration of multiple sources of sensory information. Various systematic reviews have explored the effects of SIT, specifically in children. Several reviews pertaining to children with autism spectrum disorders (ASD) indicated there was insufficient or inconclusive evidence to determine the effectiveness of SIT with this population (Case-Smith & Arbesman, 2008; National Autism Center, 2009; Parr, 2010; Tochel, 2003; Warren et al., 2011). One review (Ospina et al., 2008) stated that the evidence for sensory-motor interventions (which included SIT) was too limited or inconsistent to promote their clinical use, and another (Baranek, 2002) noted that, while SITs appeared to be safe and anecdotally have shown some benefit, the research findings are mixed. Further, Lang et al., (2012) concluded that SIT did not have a consistent positive effect as a treatment for ASD.

The Autism Advisory Committee of Atlantic Provinces Special Education Authority (APSEA), 2013 lays that behavior analytic procedures have proven efficacy across an array of behaviors including those often associated with sensory difficulties such as aggression, tantrums, self-injury, vocal and motor stereotypy. Although not all children with autism display sensory difficulties, there is evidence these types of difficulties are prevalent in this population and may interfere with performance and learning. Currently there is empirical evidence to support the use of behaviorally based interventions in the treatment of sensory differences when they interfere with learning. However, the lack of research supporting sensory integration therapy (SIT) and related sensory-based interventions places the role of these therapies in question for children with ASD. Despite the lack of evidence supporting the efficacy of SIT and related interventions, it remains a popular treatment and is still being incorporated into children's education plans. In a study conducted by Watling, Deitz, Kanny, & Mc Laughlin, in 1999, to examine the current practice patterns of occupational therapists experienced in working with children with autism spectrum disorders. a high percentage (82%) of occupational therapists surveyed reported using sensory integration as a frame of reference as well as sensory integration techniques when working with children with ASD. The paper supports the view that children with ASD process sensory information differently, but indicates the research related to the effectiveness of interventions is challenged by the complexity and variability of the disorder.

A major problem encountered in the field of autism is the children's characteristic lack of motivation. This problem is especially apparent when autistic children attempt to complete learning tasks. A study by Koegel & Egel (1979) investigated the influence of correct vs. incorrect task completion on children's motivation to respond to such tasks. Subjects were three autistic children. Results demonstrated that when subjects worked on tasks at which they were typically incorrect, their motivation for those tasks decreased to extremely low levels. However, designing treatment procedures to prompt subjects to keep responding until they completed the tasks correctly served to increase their motivation to respond to those tasks. The implications of these findings are that (a) autistic children's learning handicaps (which typically lead to low levels of correct responding) may result in few or inconsistent rewards for attempting to respond at all, thus decreasing the children's motivation; and (b) treatment procedures designed to keep the children responding until they complete a task correctly may result in coincidental reinforcement for perseverance, increasing the children's motivation to respond to those tasks.

Egel (1981) suggested that stimulus variation may influence motivation in autistics. His study investigated the effects of constant vs. varied reinforcer presentation on correct responding and on-task behavior. Results from the reversal design showed declining trends in both correct responding and on-task behavior when the same reinforcer was consistently presented, whereas, varying the reinforcers produced significantly improved and stable responding. It is quite possible that the opposite trends found during the constant and varied conditions were a function of the children's motivation. The effectiveness of the varied presentation was conceivably due to the changing sensory input the children received. In other words, the children would have been less likely to satiate on a particular reinforcer, with the result that high rates of correct responding and on-task behavior would be maintained.

Woo and Leon (2013) opined that environmental enrichment is effective in ameliorating some of the symptoms of autism in children. Given the sensorimotor deficits in most children with autism, they attempted to translate that approach to their treatment. In a randomized controlled trial, 3–12 year-old children with autism were assigned to either a sensorimotor enrichment group, which received daily olfactory/tactile stimulation along with exercises that stimulated other paired sensory modalities, or to a control group. Tests of cognitive performance and autism severity were administered to both groups at the initiation of the study and after 6 months. Severity of autism, as assessed with the Childhood Autism Rating Scale, improved significantly in the enriched group compared to controls. Forty-two percent of the enriched group and only 7% of the control group had what was considered to be a clinically significant improvement of 5 points on that scale. Sensorimotor enrichment also produced a clear improvement in cognition, as determined by their Leiter-R Visualization and Reasoning scores. Finally, 69% of parents in the enriched group and 31% of parents in the control group reported improvement in their child over the 6-month study.

Jade (2011) published a paper which comprised of a literature review and the collection of data from parents of children with autism. Data was collected and analyzed from 38 Canadian participants using an online survey to discover what parents of children with autism know about the disorder, what they understood about the outcomes of behavioral intervention and whether they felt they were receiving a comparable behavioral treatment to what they believed they should be receiving. . The results demonstrated that many parents were well-informed on current autism research, but there were a percentage of parents who still believed claims that have been well-refuted by the research. It was also discovered that many parents were not receiving the behavioral service they feel they ought to be receiving. The implications of these results are that there is still a need for extensive research with regard to quality of life for the autistic population, as well as wider dissemination of information from the scientific fields of research to the general population since they are the ones who benefit most from this knowledge.

Stephenson and Carter (2011), substantiates that an important step would be to provide teachers with current information on the state of research on multi sensory environments so that they are fully informed in their decision making. Teachers in a study conducted by Stephenson and Carter (2011) viewed educational outcomes as the critical features of use of multi sensory stimulation, as opposed to passive leisure. Given this, and that multi sensory stimulation remain an unproven intervention, a policy might be considered requiring specific measurable outcomes for all children using the technique. Nevertheless, it is a concern that considerable resources are being provided for multi sensory stimulation that could be used for the provision of evidence based interventions to students with severe disabilities.

Mann (2010) compared cognitive skills of children with autism with children who did not have the developmental disorder. Tests were given to measure the cognitive skills. The, study showed children with autism all exhibited varying patterns of cognitive strengths and weaknesses. Importantly and in contrast to other studies, many children with autism showed improvement in certain skills over time. Most of the children were better able to appreciate other's thoughts and feelings and could better regulate and control their behavior, as they grew older. These findings are immensely encouraging for parents. The study is important in that it shows instead that the cognitive skills of children with autism are not static, but change and, in most cases, improve over time. They also show that there is not one trajectory of autism.

The literature review has led to the knowhow that numerous studies have been conducted on sensory stimulation techniques and their influence on autism. However, none of them threw light into the subjective variable - strength of response from the child. It is a common notion that an autistic child's response pattern is affected, and it is well known that they respond adequately to things that elicit their interest and affection. How the subtle variations in the approach of the caregiver influences the performance level of the child demanded an exploration and are attempted in the next chapter.

3. METHOD

3.1 Design of the study

3.2 Participants and setting

3.3 Tools used for the study

3.4 Procedure

3.5 Statistical Approaches

3.1 Design of the study

Several different research methodologies are used with individuals with Autism Spectrum Disorder; each has specific advantages and disadvantages as well as quality indicators of scientific rigor. Group designs typically require random selection. Random selection requires a supportive, homogenous sample size, which is rarely present in populations with ASD. The range of symptoms and the severity across those symptoms result in a heterogeneous population and, therefore, difficulty in finding groups that are comparable. Therefore, the researcher sought for a design where randomization is not required.

Quasi-experimental designs are often used when it is difficult or impossible to use true experimental designs. Single Subject Research Designs is a quasi-experimental design where the researchers look for the effect of a treatment without using randomization. They use the "pre-post testing". This means that there are tests done before any data is collected to see if there is any person confounds or if any participants have certain tendencies. Then the actual experiment is done with posttest results recorded. This data can be compared as part of the study or the pre-test data can be included in an explanation for the actual experimental data (Thomas, Nelson & Silverman, 2011).

3.1.1 Single Subject Research

"The most advantageous approach for studying neurological conditions begins with the study of individual cases and subsequently verifying that these observations are reliably seen in other patients" (Ramachandran, 2004).

Single Subject Research Designs (also referred to as single-case experimental designs) are designs that can be applied when the sample size is one or when a number of individuals are considered as one group. These designs are typically used to study the behavioral change an individual exhibits because of some treatment. In single-subject designs, each participant serves as her or his own control, similar to a time-series design. The participant is exposed to a non-treatment and a treatment phase and performance is measured during each phase. (Gay & Airasian, 2003).

Single subject research is a repeated – measure experiment conducted on one subject i.e, the same individual is observed over time. The purpose of such repeated measurements is to determine if changes introduced in the experimental condition called intervention or treatment affect changes in the subject. To assure reliable and valid data, the measurements to be used must be clearly defined. While the focus is the individual subject, no doubt, most of these studies includes more than one subject, such as two (Best & Kahn, 1992). The focus is often on participant variability as well as average values. Those who conduct research on Single Subject Research Design look at the changes on graphs and do not analyze the results with statistics. When used with Single subjects these designs are often called A-B designs where A refers to the Baseline condition and B refers to the treatment administered (Thomas, Nelson & Silverman, 2011).

Baselines: The baseline, also called the operant level, is used to determine the status of the subject's behavior prior to the intervention by the researchers. Baseline data is often gathered by observing the different aspects of the individual's behavior. It is to be under study several times prior to the intervention. The baseline should be long enough in determining the trend of the data. Generally, three types of trends are revealed by the baseline – A stable rate, an increasing rate and decreasing rate for better evaluation of the effectiveness of intervention, the baseline must demonstrate a stable rate. If the baseline is showing an increasing rate or trend, a serious problem in evaluating the effectiveness of the intervention occurs because the baseline even prior to intervention is showing a trend in the desired direction. A good baseline is formed only after a minimum of three separate observations; however, five to eight or even more observations would be still better (Engel, 2008).

In single subject experimental research, ordinarily there are three phases – baseline, intervention, and baseline. Barlow & Hersen (1984) have opined that as far as possible, the relative length of each of the different phases should be equal, but this should not be accepted as a general direction for all situations. In fact, there may be a situation in which the first intervention has to be longer than the initial baseline in order to demonstrate an obvious change in behavior. If this happens, the subsequent phases, that is the second baseline and the second intervention should be of the same length; however, when the intervention phase is made longer, the effect of this intervention continues into the next phase (carryover effect), that is in withdrawal of the baseline.

The high degree of heterogeneity among children with ASDs poses serious challenges for researchers (National Research Council; NRC, 2001). Research group designs, which compare two seemingly separate but equal groups of participants, are difficult to conduct with individuals with ASD and are used less frequently than single-subject research designs (SSRDs). Also, given that intensive early intervention is recommended for individuals with autism (Interagency Autism Coordinating Committee; IACC, 2011), there are ethical considerations to think about if one group is placed in a treatment condition while leaving a second group in a no-treatment condition.

One of the most commonly used types of SSRD in autism research is the multiple-baseline design (NRC, 2001).

3.1.2 Multiple Baseline Design

The multiple baseline design is the most widely used experimental design for evaluating treatment defects in applied behavior analysis. A highly flexible tactic enables researchers and practitioners to analyze the effects of an independent variable across multiple behaviors, settings, and/or subjects without having to withdraw the treatment variable to verify that the improvements in behavior were a direct result of the application of the treatment.

Bear, Wolf, and Risley (1968) first described the multiple baseline design in the applied behavior analysis literature. They presented the multiple baseline design as an alternative to the reversal design for two situations: (a) when the target behavior is likely to be irreversible, or (b) when it is undesirable, impractical or unethical to reverse conditions.

The multiple baseline design takes three basic forms:

- Across behaviors design – consisting of two or more different behaviors of the same subject.
- Across setting design – consisting of the same behavior of the same subject in two or more different settings, situations or periods.
- Across subjects design – consisting of the same behavior of two or more different participants.

<u>**Multiple baselines across behaviors design**</u>: Multiple baselines across behaviors design begins with the concurrent measurements of two or more behaviors of the single participant. After steady state responding has been obtained under baseline conditions, the investigator applies the independent variable to one of the behaviors while maintaining baseline

conditions for the other behavior(s). When steady state of criterion level performance has been reached for the first behavior, the independent variable is applied to the next behavior, and so on (e.g., Bell, Yong, Salzberg, & West, 1991; Gena, Krantz, McClanahan, & Poulson, 1996; Higgins, Williams & McLaughlin, 2001).

Like all experimental tactics, the multiple baseline design requires the researcher to make certain assumptions about how the behavior – environment relations under investigation function, even though discovering the existence and operation of those relations is the very reason for conducting the research.

The present study uses multiple baselines across behaviors design to examine the trends in the motor, communicative and cognitive skills of two children with autism following intervention. The "behaviors" studied are part of the intervention program implemented.

3.2. Participants and setting

Statistics state that autism occurs, 4.3 times more often in boys than girls. Hence, it was deemed worthwhile to conduct the study on boys to gather a more representative information. The chosen subjects were four boys with a reported diagnosis of Autism. The researcher, a trained behavior therapist in autism management, had been working as psychologist in an institute for cognitive and communication disorder management in Kerala for six years.

As the study commenced, enquiry was made about autistic children below 12 years who might benefit from sensory stimulation techniques that could be integrated into the child's day. Various centers in the district were contacted which provided service to Autistics with the request to nominate a child who fulfilled the following criteria:

Inclusion criteria:

- he must be a clinically diagnosed autistic within the age group 6 -12 yrs,
- he must be receiving special education services in some capacity,
- he must exhibit some behavioral challenges.

Exclusion criteria:

- The child should not be having physical handicaps or sensory disabilities like, blindness or deafness
- The child should not be having Seizure Disorder.

It was put in a popular daily newspaper that clients are required. Institutions seldom permit to conduct intervention on their clients, and the researcher being a non – practicing therapist at the time of the research, had a hard time finding the subjects. Ultimately, nine clients conceded.

Once the interested clients were obtained, the next step was a formative assessment to choose from them the appropriate sample for the present study. The children fulfilling the Inclusion/ Exclusion criteria had to be chosen. The design of the study does not require a control group as such, because in Single Subject Research Design the subject serves as his or her own control. However, it also needs to be mentioned that the subjects under study were attending a special education program and were given speech therapy. In order to rule out the effect of the other therapies and its possible influence on the children, a control group was also taken.

Out of the nine clients whose parents were willing to cooperate with the intervention program, four boys were chosen. All the four participants were attending a special school in the district. The children were matched and paired based on age, date of admission to the school (duration of special care), severity of Autism rating, and sensory sensitivity/ sensory preferences.

It was ensured that (if found effective) the intervention procedure shall be introduced to the control group also after three months.

3.2.1. The Participants

The participants in the experimental group were Aman and Sam (Pseudo named)

- <u>Participant no. 1 - Aman</u> was an 8 yr old boy admitted to the school in October 2009 with a diagnosis of Childhood autism. He hailed from a middle class family and was the single child of a non-consanguineous couple. The father is in government service and the mother, a homemaker. As per the clinical reports, Aman was moderately autistic and severely retarded in social functioning at the time the study began.

- <u>Participant no. 2 - Sam</u> was a 6 yr old boy admitted to the school in February 2012 with a diagnosis of Childhood autism. He is one of a fraternal twin, belonging to an affluent family. The parents - a non-consanguineous couple, were overly religious and superstitious, yet passive in the management of Sam. Father is an Engineer in a well known multinational company and mother, a well-educated homemaker. Sam was diagnosed as having severe autism, and retardation in social functioning at the time the study began.

Two children who matched the experimental pair were also chosen as the pair to be observed. They were John and Roshan.

- <u>Participant no. 3 - John</u> was an 8 yr old boy admitted to the school in April 2009 with a diagnosis of Childhood autism. He hailed from a middle class family and was the elder of two children of a non-consanguineous couple. Both parents are in government service. As per the clinical reports, he was moderately autistic and moderately retarded in social functioning at the time of the study.

- **Participant no. 4 - Roshan** was a 7 yr old kid with severe autism and moderate retardation in social functioning. He was admitted to the school in November 2011. Roshan also hailed from a family of upper middle class economic status. He was the only child of his parents who were in their forties. Both are well educated and employed.

3.2.2 Observer in the study

The psychologist who had been a newly recruited trainee in the school was the observer in the study. She was also taking individual behavior modification sessions for the two children subjected to intervention. The rest of the children were attended to by the researcher as well as the observer, in the combined sessions, group sessions or play sessions. The intervention was done strictly in the format suggested by the researcher and the behavior measurement taken subsequently.

Collecting behavior data in applied setting requires attention, keen judgment and perseverance. The observer in the study was given training regarding the measurement of the behaviors subjected to study. Practice sessions were taken with other clients before the actual data collection.

3.2.3 Setting and Time

The study was conducted in the school premises as well as a therapy room. The therapy room is a 15 x 10 feet room, adequately ventilated and curtained. Intervention was made thrice a week, for one hour. The control group also was attended to in the same frequency and duration but not intervened. The study was conducted for three months, from April to June 2012.

3.3. Tools used for the study

3.3.1 Vineland's Social Maturity Scale (VSMS)

Vineland Social Maturity Scale (VSMS) was developed by Doll in 1935. Malin (1992) did the Indian adaptation. The VSMS gives an index of the child's social & adaptive development and yields a Social Quotient. The Indian adaptation charts development until 15 years of age. Correlation coefficients ranging from 0.85 – 0.96 have been obtained from a sample of children with normal development.

3.3.2 Childhood Autism Rating Scale (CARS)

Schopler, Reichler and Renner (1999) developed the Childhood Autism Rating Scale (CARS). The Childhood Autism Rating Scale (CARS) is a 15-item observation rating scale developed to identify children with Autism aged 2 years and above, and to distinguish them from developmentally handicapped children without the autism syndrome. It further distinguishes children with autism in the mild/moderate/severe range. The test-retest reliability indicated a correlation of .88, and a criterion related validity coefficient of .88 indicating that the CARS results are in agreement with expert clinical judgments.

3.3.3 The Sensory Integration Inventory (SII-R)

The Sensory Integration Inventory-Revised (SII-R; Reisman & Hanschu, 1992) is a non-standardized checklist that can be used to screen and rule out serious maladaptive behaviors that are not due to sensory dysfunction. The SII-R can be completed in less than 30 minutes by an Occupational therapist who knows the client well. Alternatively, it can be used to interview a client's teacher or parent. Items are separated into four categories (tactile, vestibular, proprioceptive, general reactions) and are answered by checking "yes," "no," or "unsure" based on the typical response of the client. It is not standardized; therefore, the therapist must look for patterns of response that may indicate dysfunction in sensory integration. The authors report that the SII-R screens out individuals who have serious behaviors for reasons other than sensory integration dysfunction. The Inventory is divided into sections associated with sensory integrative processing: tactile, vestibular, proprioceptive, and general reactions. In each section, behaviors suggestive of sensory needs are listed as well as the self-stimulatory or self-injurious behavior associated with that system. The evaluator indicates whether or not these behaviors have been observed. A profile of sensory strengths and needs and associated self-injurious and self-stimulating behaviors is elicited through this process that provides a guideline for treatment.

The SII-R was originally developed with a group of adults with cognitive disabilities, but therapists have found it to be useful with a variety of clients who cannot fully cooperate in a testing situation – from children with Autism to adults with schizophrenia or Alzheimer's. One of the major advantages of the SII-R is the cluster of self-stimulatory items listed for each of the sensory areas. Since children with Autism have been reported to exhibit increased sensory stimulation behaviors, the SII-R can be helpful due to its ability to illustrate that self-stimulatory behaviors may be sensory based. If numerous self-stimulatory behaviors are found within one sensory system versus another, the probable cause for the self-stimulation is sensory related.

For the comparison of profiles, the scores are entered as percentage of sensitivity in each area.

3.3.4 Curriculum Guide for autistic children

Although formal assessments can be useful in the initial diagnosis and eligibility process, the use of informal developmental scales and curriculum based assessments (CBAs) can often provide a more authentic and accurate assessment of a student's ability across a variety of environments and settings. Curriculum-based assessments provide an assessment of an individual's learning style, preferences, strengths, and needs. Additionally, these tools can be used to document progress toward mastery of learning objectives. In the study, the activities listed in the 'Beginning Curriculum Guide' given in 'Behavioral Intervention for Young Children with Autism' (Maurice, 1996) was used. Twenty items were selected to check for the status of the four children. The module provides a chronological pattern of activities that shall be introduced and worked upon children with autism. Those activities that the child could not perform would be chosen as the tasks to be intervened (Virginia Department of Education, 2010).

A mixed-method curriculum is used to recognize a student's readiness, language, learning style, and interests. A mixed curriculum is built around existing general curriculum and included teachers' alterations, modifications and enhancements.

3.4. Procedure

3.4.1 Case history and Assessments

No one should do much of anything with a child with autism until having some very basic background information on the child. The assessments included a detailed history taking from the parent, status evaluation by the psychologist, the special educator, the speech therapist and occupational therapist who served for the institute.

3.4.1.1. Participant no. 1 - Aman

Aman is the single child of a non-consanguineous couple. The father is a government service man and the mother, a homemaker. Reportedly, the parents noticed a language delay in the baby by two and a half years of age. He was taken to the Child Development Centre, Trivandrum as per the Pediatrician's advice. There he was initially diagnosed as having Childhood Autism, with hypothyroidism. Since then the boy was under medication to maintain the hormone balance. He was admitted to the special school where the study was conducted in 2009.

Aman could not chew food and had difficulty in swallowing also. Therefore, the parents gave him only milk and porridge. As he was having hypothyroidism, the parents consulted a physician to rule out presence of nodules in the gland, which usually made swallowing difficulty and he was reported asymptomatic. The physician considered it as a case of functional dysphagia – having no organic cause.

Aman was very sensitive emotionally and broke down to tears at the slightest provocation. Speech was meager and he would lead the parent to the objects that he needed and would point to.

Family history showed maternal hypothyroidism. Mother had two miscarriages before the issue. She was under medication when pregnant and was on Levothyroxin, when the study commenced.

Birth history: *prenatal:* Other than the hormonal imbalance, no other issues were reported during the prenatal period.

Perinatal: normal delivery. Baby cried immediately and weighed 3kg.

Postnatal: uneventful. Baby was breast fed and healthy.

Developmental history: Onset of speech was delayed. By around two years, Aman said 'ma'. A few other words also were spoken later. Now he uttered sounds to seek attention but meaningful speech was absent. Motor milestones were normally achieved.

Behavioral Assets and deficits: By around three years, the parents noticed that the child did not speak age adequately. Communication by other means was also very less. He would make peculiar noises and was weepy. He preferred to be alone. Feeding the boy was the most dreadful thing for the parents. He would spit out and gag if forced to eat. He was again taken to the Child Development Centre, and on the advice of the developmental therapists, enrolled him in a special school.

Immunization history: Complete.

Schooling: Aman was sent to a kindergarten for 2 years from where he was referred to the special school.

Tests given

a. Vineland's Social Maturity Scale (VSMS) yielded a score of 34 as his Social Quotient, which suggested that his social functioning was equivalent to 2 yrs 7 months, which is a severely retarded state.

b. Childhood Autism Rating Scale (CARS) yielded a score of 36.5 placing him in the moderate level of autism.

c. The Sensory Integration Inventory (SII-R) assessed by the Occupational therapist showed that Aman had issues in fifteen areas out of twenty-four, covering six domains. Figure 1 shows the Sensory profile of first participant. He was having severe complaints with oral sensitivity, personal space, and motor skills stimulating the visual and proprioceptive senses.

d. Curriculum Guide for autistic children The assessment was done by the researcher after enquiring the details with parents and special educator. Reportedly, Aman could do four out of the initial 20 tasks chosen from the curriculum.

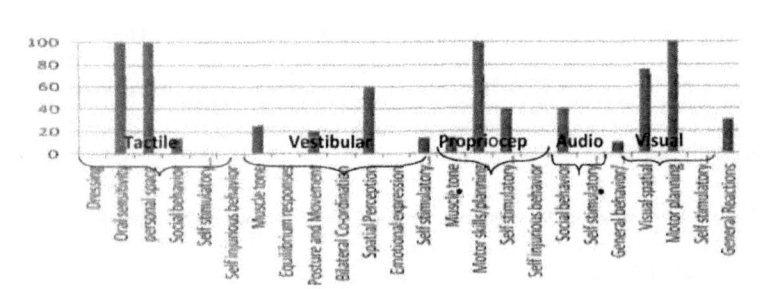

Figure 1 Sensory profile of the first participant

3.4.1.2. Participant no. 2 - Sam

Sam's parents noticed lack of eye contact and irritability much earlier- by one and half years. As there was a sibling (twin), they could clearly find the deviation in the boy's developmental profile. He was always irritated and whining. No sucking reflex was there. He was weepy all through the night when he was a baby. Sam had an irritable bowel and suffered from constipation. The parents took much care to regulate his diet by giving raw papaya, salads and plenty of water; still it seemed an unmanageable issue. Every three days the parents had to give laxatives to clear the bowel. The boy would behave much calmer the following day.

By, three years, the boy was noticed as not speaking adequately. He used the words 'papa', and 'Tata' rarely but never repeated words after two and half years. Sam keeps on staring into the space or spins self. Sam had swallowing difficulty (dysphagia). He kept his lips shut tight. He hated chewing and did not let anybody brush his teeth. He does not rinse his mouth but simply spits out.

Family history: Mother is epileptic since 14 yrs of age and is still on anti epileptic drugs. The paternal grandfather is reportedly having mental illness.

Birth history: *Prenatal:* Other than the issue mentioned above, no other issues were reported in the prenatal period.

Perinatal: Normal delivery. Baby cried immediately and weighed normal

Postnatal: uneventful. He was not breast-fed.

Developmental history: Speech milestones: First word was uttered by one and half years of age. Later it regressed and now he is mute. Motor milestones were slow. He had at least two months delay in all milestones when compared with the twin.

Behavioral Assets and deficits: By two years, he was taken to a centre for corrective therapy to improve his communication. There he was diagnosed as Autistic. Sam did not co-operate with the sessions and hence the program was discontinued. Feeding the boy was the most dreadful thing for the parents. He would gulp rice and dal, corn flakes and milk if forced to eat. The parent reported that his play behavior was appropriate to that of his twin brother. They run around and tumble up in bed in the evenings. Peer group interaction was poor.

Immunization history: Complete

Schooling: Sam was sent to a kindergarten for 2 years from where he was referred to the special school.

Tests given

a. Vineland's Social Maturity Scale (VSMS) yielded a score of 26 as his Social Quotient, which showed that his social functioning as equivalent to 1 yrs 6 months, which is a severely retarded state.

b. Childhood Autism Rating Scale (CARS) yielded a score of 45.5 placing him in the severe level of autism.

c. The Sensory Integration Inventory (SII-R) assessed by the Occupational therapist showed that he had issues in seventeen areas out of twenty-four, which spanned six domains. Figure 2 shows the Sensory profile of Second participant. High level of sensitivity was shown in oral stimulation, bilateral co –ordination, spatial perception, emotional expression and visual motor planning.

d. Curriculum Guide for autistic children: The assessment was done by the researcher after enquiring to the parents and special educator. Reportedly, Sam could not do any of the initial 20 tasks chosen from the curriculum.

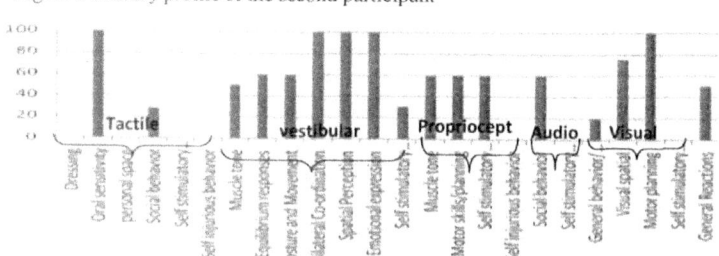

Figure 2 Sensory profile of the second participant

3.4.1.3. Participant no. 3 -. John

He is the elder of two siblings. Parents reported him as hyperactive even from the time he started walking. They noticed delay in speech also. The pediatrician suggested speech therapy to which the parents obliged to. Later it was noticed that he showed motor stereotypic movements as arraying things and spinning wheels. During such situations, he becomes so engrossed in activities that he is detached from others.

Family history: no relevant issues were observed in the family history

Birth history: *prenatal:* uneventful

    Perinatal: Full term normal delivery. Baby cried immediately and weighed normal

    Postnatal : uneventful.

Developmental history: Speech milestones: First word was uttered by one year. Now he uses two word phrases and echolalic speech. Motor milestones were normal.

Behavioral assets and deficits: John is so wiggly and throws tantrums when forced to do any activities. He screams aloud at times. By three years, he was taken to a centre for speech therapy to improve his communication. There he was diagnosed as Autistic.

Immunization history: Complete.

Schooling: John was sent to a kindergarten from 3 years of age. According to parents, he would adapt well in any setting but was restless. The parents came to know about the special school and brought him there in 2009.

Tests given

a. Vineland's Social Maturity Scale (VSMS) yielded a score of 42 as his Social Quotient, which showed that his social functioning is equivalent to 3 yrs 7 months, which is a moderately retarded state.

b. Childhood Autism Rating Scale (CARS) yielded a score of 35 placing him in the moderate level of autism.

c. The Sensory Integration Inventory (SII-R) assessed by the Occupational therapist shows that he has issues in fifteen areas out of twenty-four, covering six domains. Figure 3. shows the Sensory profile of the third participant. Severe issues are noticed in the personal space and motor skills stimulating proprioceptive sense.

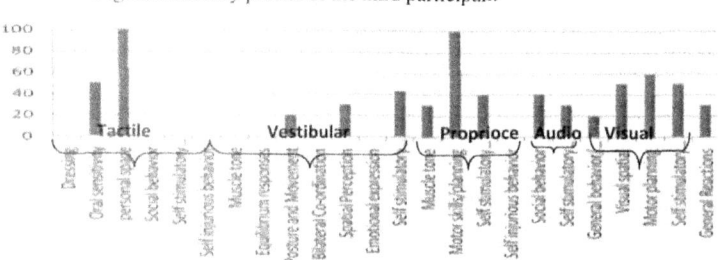

Figure 3 Sensory profile of the third participant

c. Curriculum Guide for autistic children: The assessment was done by the researcher after enquiring to the parents and special educator. Reportedly, John could do 5 out of the initial 20 tasks chosen from the curriculum.

3.4.1.4. Participant no.4 - Roshan

Roshan is a single child. The parents reported that the boy was conceived after multiple issues of miscarriage and treatments. By one and half years, they noticed the child showing stereotyped motor movements as hand flapping. Speech was absent. The pediatrician referred the child to Child Development Centre, Thiruvananthapuram. After four months of intervention by the developmental therapist, he started to speak. Roshan was taken to several doctors and was subjected to multitude of treatments before he was brought to the school.

Family history: Paternal and maternal ages were 40 and 37 when the child was conceived. They had undergone infertility treatment also prior to this child was born.

Birth history: *Prenatal:* uneventful

Perinatal: Full term Caesarian delivery. Baby cried immediately and weighed normal

Postnatal: uneventful.

Developmental history: Speech milestones: First word was uttered by three years. Now he uses two word phrases though echolalic speech is present. Motor milestones were delayed.

Behavioral assets and deficits: His compulsive pacing up and down is managed by the Special educator. He maintains eye contact but does not prefer anybody going near.

Immunization history: Complete.

Schooling: Roshan was not sent to any other schools before being in the present school.

Tests given

a. Vineland's Social Maturity Scale (VSMS) yielded a score of 42 as his Social Quotient, which shows that his social functioning is equivalent to 2 yrs 7 months, which is a moderately retarded state.

b. Childhood Autism Rating Scale (CARS) yielded a score of 42 placing him in the severe level of autism.

c. The Sensory Integration Inventory (SII-R) assessed by the Occupational therapist showed that he has issues in seventeen areas out of twenty-four, across six domains. Figure 4. shows the sensory profile of fourth participant. High level of sensitivity is shown in spatial perception, emotional expression and visual motor planning.

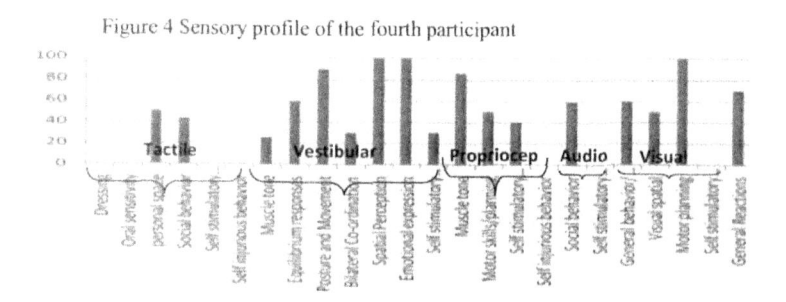

Figure 4 Sensory profile of the fourth participant

d. Curriculum Guide for autistic children: The assessment was done by the researcher after enquiring to the parents and special educator. As per their reports, Roshan could do five out of the initial 20 tasks chosen from the curriculum.

3.4.2 Data collection

Once the assessments were complete, it was decided that the children Aman and Sam shall be subjected to intervention. All the tests given above were used to match the groups. Aman and John (participants 1 and 3) as well as Sam and Roshan (participants 2 and 4) were matched for age, gender, severity of Autism and year of admission to the school.

An intervention plan had to be prepared in order to delineate the tasks and present them in the intended format of multisensory stimulation. Tasks were chosen by the researcher after discussing with the observer. Those tasks that the children failed to achieve in the tests due to lack of opportunity were also considered for intervention. In addition, the activities mentioned in the Curriculum Guide that the child could not achieve are also included.

The tasks were listed out in such a way that they form a tier of three activities- one that predominantly stimulates the motor activity, communication and cognition. It was taken care of to combine at least one motor, communicative and cognitive task in a session (Notated as M, C and G*). The task was numbered in order to facilitate identification.

For example: the sixth tier of activities given to Aman

M6 -   Deep breathing   – task primarily focusing Motor skills

C6 -   Wh – questions   – task primarily focusing Communication

G6 -   Picture Identification   – task primarily focusing Cognition

Multiple baseline designs of three to five tiers are most common. When the effects of the independent variable are substantial and reliably replicated, a three or four tier multiple baseline design provides a convincing demonstration of experimental effect. The more replications one conducts, the more convincing the demonstrations will be (Cooper, Heron & Heward, 2014).

*as communication and cognition may get confused

3.4.2.1. Measuring Behavior

Measurement is "the process of assigning numbers and units to particular features of objects or events. It involves attaching a number representing the observed extent of a dimensional quality to an appropriate unit. The number and the unit together constitute the measure of the object or event" (Johnston & Penny Packer, 1993). The researcher's ability to achieve a scientific understanding of behavior depends on her ability to measure it.

Behavior can be measured using

- Fundamental measures (as repeatability, temporal extent, and temporal locus) or
- Derived measures (as percentage and trials to criterion) or by

- Definitional measures (as form and intensity).

Neither form nor intensity of responding (magnitude) is a fundamental dimensional quality of behavior, but each is an important quantitative parameter for defining and verifying the occurrence of many response classes.

3.4.2.1.1. Magnitude: Measuring the Response Strength

Magnitude refers to the force or intensity with which a response is emitted. The desired outcomes of some behaviors are contingent on responding at or above (or below) a certain intensity or force (Cooper et al., 2014).. This is used to determine whether responses that meet magnitude criteria; responses that meet those criteria are measured and reported by one or more fundamental or derivative measures (e.g. Count of responses meeting magnitude criteria). It is an important measure when desired outcome of behavior is contingent on responses within certain range of magnitudes.

In the study, a Likert five point scale is prepared for scoring the strength of the elicited response. It is uni polar (ranges from "no response at all" to "independent"). The lowest level of response is a blank response or if the child responded in an unrelated manner as if to communicate his disinterest.

Repeated measures are taken for assessing the responses made by the subject, for a particular task, within a session and across four to six sessions. Persistent prompting might be needed for autistic people in executing a task in one attempt. In the study, if a task seems curbing irritability the number of attempts made is reduced, otherwise four deliberate efforts are made. Two to four attempts are given for a particular activity in a session - baseline and intervention.

The score was given for the best of the trials within a session. It was also planned to present the task in a random order (motor, communicative and cognitive tasks).

Prompting Hierarchy

Prompting hierarchy provides a systematic method of assessing a participant's learning and level of independence. The method used here is "Most-To-Least" Prompting. This is simply using a very high level of support (prompting) when teaching a new skill, and then systematically fading down to lower level prompts as the child masters the skill. Thus, the prompting sequence is:

- Physical Assistance
- Verbal Assistance
- Independent response (No assistance)

Response hierarchy

By response hierarchy, the researcher refers to a way of observing the interest evolving in a child because of the therapeutic approach. It is commonly observed in schools that the children are complacent and respond so mechanically or passively to certain commands from authority figures. Autistic people have the tendency not to respond when they are not interested. The therapist has to be sensitive to the subtle variations in the readiness, preferences and inclination shown by the child towards the activities that are introduced.

Evidence is emerging; however, to suggest that incorporating the interests of children with autism spectrum disorders into interventions with the children might have positive effects and consequences (Boyd, Alter, & Conroy, 2005). Renninger (2000) differentiated between two types of interests (personal and situational) Personal interests refer to the personal characteristics of an individual that engages him or her in preferred or enjoyable activities. for example, preference for certain objects, activities, and actions; Situational interests refer to the characteristics of a child's social or nonsocial environment that evoke engagement with people or material. This includes the interest for people, objects, activities, etc. that evoke and sustain attention and sustained engagement (Chen, Darst, & Pangrazi, 2001). With increase in interest, the level of performance also varies.

The ultimate aim is a spontaneous response from a child when the stimulus is presented. Spontaneous communication is defined as communicative behaviors that occur in the absence of prompts, instructions or other verbal cues. Learning characteristics that must be considered in spontaneous communication include the motivational variables (Lovaas & Smith, 1989; Rogers & Pennington, 1991). Spontaneous initiations are therefore necessary for individuals with ASD to be judged as socially competent during communicative exchanges (Wetherby & Prutting, 1984).

It can generally be agreed that individuals with ASD rely on prompts to evoke expressive communication (Chiang, 2009) hence; a response hierarchy is made from the most prompted as well as least responded condition to spontaneous response condition. A score of one through five is assigned to the improvement in response pattern noticed. The response hierarchy and scoring is entered in Table 1.

Table 1. The response hierarchy and scoring

Pattern of response	Score
Blank response or responds in an unrelated manner	1
Passive Attempt with Physical Prompting	2
Passive attempt with Verbal Prompt / Active attempt with Physical Prompt	3
Active response with Verbal Prompt	4
Independent/ spontaneous response without prompting	5

3.4.3. The Behavior Modification Program and Scoring

When a client enters a treatment room, the therapist must be prepared to respond in a variety of ways simultaneously: Immediately engaging in a dialogue with the client, during which we listen, observe and communicate, learn about the client's readiness to begin the treatment session and the state of his central nervous system (Fisher, Murray & Bundy, 1991). Once the child arrives, having a structured task involving controlled movement may assist in regulation of activity level. He may have completed the morning routine of waking, eating, dressing, and transitioning to school in a highly aroused state with very poor ability to focus on a visual motor activity requiring attention and has to try hard to inhibit the extraneous stimuli (auditory and tactile as well as emotional arousal).

A client demonstrates his or her motivation to do an activity by becoming totally involved in it. If the activity is too hard for a young child and if we do not react quickly enough to alter the demands of the task, the child may become frustrated or discouraged. It may then be difficult to reengage the child during that treatment session and possibly during subsequent sessions (Fisher et al., 1991). For the current research purpose an intervention plan is made according to the child's skills and interests. If a client expresses either verbally or nonverbally that he does not want to perform an activity, we must seek to discern the reason for this apparent lack of motivation, since the cause suggests the remedy. Therefore it was decided to make changes in the listed activities if the child did not comply or found a task exceptionally tiresome or difficult.

Moving fluidly from one activity to another results in a treatment session that looks and feels playful. To the untrained observer this may appear to be less structured than are other kinds of intervention programs. Parents and teachers sometimes misinterpret the playful nature of the treatment session and question the validity of the intervention (Fisher et al., 1991). It is therefore important to express clearly the purpose of the treatment activities and the benefits of playful and fluid sessions to the important others in the client's life. A session typically involves several segments during which language, play and social skills are targeted with both structured and unstructured interactions. None of these techniques are new; rather they are time tested, common sense techniques which have been used by other caregivers for years.

Figures of a few assistive devices used in the treatment program are also given along with for the interested readers.

3.4.3.1. Participant 1 - Aman

Intervention plan

The intervention plan for the first participant for three months is shown in Table 2

Activities assigned for each session (as per the intervention plan), the multisensory assistance given and the score provided by the researcher for the participant's response are detailed below.

Table.2 Intervention plan for the first participant for three months

Activity /Session	1	2	3	4	5	6	7	8	9	10	11	12	13	14	15	16	17	18	19	20	21	22	23	24	25	26	27	28	29	30	31	32	33	34	35	36	37	38	39	40
M1 Jumping	B	B	B	B																																				
C1 Hello/Handshake	B	B	B	B	B	B	B	B	I	I	I	I																												
G1 Scribbling	B	B	B	B	B	B	B	B	B	B	B	B	I	I	I	I																								
M2 Blowing					B	B	B	B	B	B	B	B	I																											
C2 Give & take									B	B	B	B	B	I	I	I	I																							
G2 Dot to dot													B	B	B	B	B																							
M3 Tongue movt.																				I																				
C3 Action chain														B	B	B	B	B	B	B																				
G3 Peg board																			I	I	I	I	I																	
M4 Gum movt.														B	B	B	B	B	B	B																				
C4 Respond to call																	B	B	B	B	I	I	I	I																
G4 Draw in 4 dirn.																	B	B	B	B	I	I	B	B	I	I	I	I												
M5 Sipping																	B	B	B	B																				
C5 Identify people																					B	B	B	B	I	I	I	I												
G5 Draw shapes																					B	B	B	B	B	B	B	B	B	B	B	B								
M6 Deep breathe																					B	B	B	B																
C6 Whose?																									B	B	B	B	B	B	B	B								
G6 Picture Idntfctn																													I	I	I	I	I	I	I	I				
M7 Descend																													I	I	I	I								
C7 Yes/ No gesture																													B	B	B	B		I	I	I				
G7 Writing																																	B	B	B	B	I	I	I	I

B-Baseline
I- Intervention

Session #1

BASE LINE			INTERVENTION
M1	Jumping	1	-
C1	Hello/Handshake	2	-
G1	Scribbling	2	-

Every human being has a basic and natural desire to be acknowledged as significant and some of this significance can be given by greeting them properly.

Hello/ Handshake: Aman did not make eye contact when met for the first time. He was sniffing his fingers after touching the table and sat on his chair with a downward gaze.

A glance from a familiar person, an outstretched hand to shake, and an approaching person, are ways people engage in conversations. These 'pre-greeting' behaviors may be understood naturally by some children but other children may need direct instruction in this area. When an initial greeting was given – a warm, loud enough - "Hi Aman!" he pulled his chair to the far end of the room without lifting his gaze. I went up to him, took his hands in mine lightly, and said Hello Aman. Then he said "allo". This seemed, his way of saying Hello.

Jumping: The task intends to provide joint compression input, enhance alertness and acts as energy release for kids (DoDea, 2002).

"Aman would you **jump**? **Jump for me?**" He did not respond.

I paused for a few seconds before proceeding to the next task, not knowing whether the silence might be the response latency of the kid. It is important to give individuals with ASD a little extra time to respond (latency), in order to process information. When no signs of response occurred, I proceeded to the next task.

Scribbling: The act of scribbling can serve small muscle coordination and the control improves with practice, cognitive abilities are exercised, and the physical movements provide emotional release.

A paper was placed before him and a box of wax crayons.

"OK! Shall we **draw**?" No response

"You like **coloring**?" No response. He kept on fidgeting and made faintly audible vocal stereotypic sounds.

The coloring prompts when repeated for a third time, he picked up one crayon sniffed it, gave a quick lick and made a scribble – a stroke on the paper kept before him. The passive attempt with prompting was scored '2'. The prompts did not yield a response for Jumping and the task was scored '1'. For the passive response made with physical prompting for 'Hello' a score of '2' is given.

A bottle of milk was send every day for Aman by the parents to give to him in between the sessions, as it was the only food he took! When given, he opens the bottle and pours a mouthful; the bottle not touching his lips. The milk is held in the mouth for a long time. He takes it very slowly or else somebody has to ask him to swallow. The gulping went on in the same procedure for twenty-one sessions when it was intervened.

Session # 2, 3 and 4

In order to confine to the requirements of the research design no attempts were made to alter the response pattern of the child for three more consecutive sessions. The performance of the child also was stable across these sessions.

Session # 5

	BASE LINE			INTERVENTION	
M2	Blowing	1	M1	Jumping	2
C1	Hello/Handshake	2		-	
G1	Scribbling	2		-	

After a week when Aman came in, the usual 'Hello Aman!' was said, to which he did not respond. When I went closer and held his hands, he would not even mould his palm to grasp mine, but he says 'allo' softly. For the passive response made with physical prompting for 'Hello' a score of '2' is given.

It was noticed that the institution had a trampoline- as shown in Figure 5 seldom used! It was pulled down to the room and I started jumping on it. A rhyme "jump, jump, jump, and jump up high..." was sung along with the rhythm of the jumps. Aman wondered what was happening. He promptly came up to the device and extended his hands to me. He was clutching my hands tightly when helped to climb on the device. When I said, "come on Aman, **jump** with me" I could see him scared to jump. Therefore, I stood on the trampoline and made him sense the swing (up – down swing) of the device. For the passive response made with physical prompting for 'Jumping' a score of '2' is given.

Figure 5. Assistive device used - Trampoline.

Once he made positive approximations it was difficult to withhold multisensory prompting for the other two tasks viz. C1 and G1. Since the baselines are still being measured, they had to be held constant. The other two tasks are measured in the set format.

After the jumping session, he was settled down with cognition tasks. Seated in his chair behind a table, Aman was given the color pencil box and paper. The usual verbal prompt was given. He was pre occupied with the 'jumping' and kept on humming and pointing to the trampoline. When persistent prompts were given for coloring, he made a few quick vague strokes in the paper. The passive attempt with prompting was scored '2'. The stroke made was a quick one as he was eager to get back to his preferred activity. I counted on that...an urge is created!

Blowing: Aman had high oral sensitivity and hence the occupational therapist advised to incorporate the task. Actions of the lips, jaw, tongue, soft palate, larynx, and respiratory muscles that are intended to influence the physiologic underpinnings of the oropharyngeal mechanism improve its functions. They include active muscle exercise, muscle stretching, passive exercise, and sensory stimulation (McCauley, Strand, Lof, Schooling, & Frymark, 2009).

A candle was lit and the therapist blew it off. Aman was watching. "would you **blow**? Aman, shall we **blow**?" The candle was lit again. Aman was looking at the whole event but did not blow. He was scored '1' for no response.

Session # 6

	BASE LINE			INTERVENTION	
M2	Blowing	2	M1	Jumping	3
C1	Hello/Handshake	2		-	
G1	Scribbling	2		-	

Aman came in with more enthusiasm, gave me a quick 'knowing' smile and immediately I made the hailing 'Hello Aman!' No response to that. He went directly to the trampoline. He promptly came back, pulled out a chair for himself and sat down to remove his shoes! So he wanted to sense it bare footed! Nevertheless, the shoelace was tightly knotted. He made one or two lame attempts to release the knot. When failed he peered through the corner of his eyes to check whether help was around. As he felt that I was not paying attention to what he did, he came to me, pulled my hands to his shoelace, and hummed. I came closer and stretched my hand saying 'Hello Aman!' He was too engaged now to respond to that. Then I took his palm in mine and said 'Hello' to which he said the usual soft 'allo'. (Scored '2'). I removed the shoes and he climbed on the trampoline. Aman held out his hands for support (active attempt with physical prompting was scored '3'). He was cheered well for the efforts made. The rhyme was sung to keep it rhythmic. It was noted that the music did not irritate him.

The teacher had told that Aman was most irritable during the music hours, when a teacher would sing out classics for the kids. His vocal stereotypies were quite unmanageable then. Aman would keep on making weird sounds and clapped aloud to shut out the stimuli.

Scribbling: After 10 minutes of jumping, he was settled down to drawing. He picked up a crayon quickly, I expected a scribbling and he threw it away to which I made the first '**No**'.

("No throwing away! OK!"). It was an audible, clear, firm NO but not an intimidating one. Immediately I took back the thrown away crayon. He was looking at my reaction, when I managed to give a smile and a caressing on his shoulder. I could see his lips twitching to hide a smile! After repeated physical prompts, Aman made a few scribbles on the paper. He was given a score of two.

Blowing: When the candle was lit, he turned away his head 2 - 3 times. Ultimately a sound was elicited which sounded like the blow I made. Nevertheless, Aman opened his mouth and said 'ooh' all the while he was fidgeting and restless: scored '2'. He was mimicking the sound but the breath was taken 'in'. Aman was well applauded for that though it was a failed venture.

Session # 7

	BASE LINE			INTERVENTION	
M2	Blowing	2	M1	Jumping	3
C1	Hello/Handshake	2		-	
G1	Scribbling	2		-	

Aman came to the room by himself (otherwise, he is led to the room by the caretaker). He gave a fleeting eye contact and went to his seat. When the greeting was given, he paused on the way. I took his hand and said Hello, thrice to which he responded the soft 'allo': scored '2'.

Scribbling continued in the same on/ off mode: score '2'

Blowing also elicited the same breath in response hence scored '2'.

For ***jumping***, he would climb on the trampoline after removing shoes, extent his arms for my support as well as waiting for the rhyme: scored '3'. Jumping was getting more willful. The shoes as well as the socks were tight fitted and were difficult to wear and remove. Therefore, the parent was given a feed back to change the footwear.

Session # 8

	BASE LINE			INTERVENTION	
M2	Blowing	2	M1	Jumping	4
C1	Hello/Handshake	2		-	
G1	Scribbling	2		-	

Aman rushed in to the room by himself. He gave the fleeting eye contact and went to his seat. After the greeting was given (several times), he made the soft 'allo': Scored '2'.

Scribbling continued in the same mode: scored '2'.

Blowing also elicited the same breath in response: scored '2'.

It was noticed Aman removed shoes all by himself. It was a new pair of well fitting shoe and socks. (He was so eager to jump and no attention was paid to his plea for help to remove them). When climbed on the trampoline he extended hands for support. His hands were held occasionally. Meanwhile, the kid was being verbally prompted. It was noticed that he started enjoying the bouncing instead of the swinging. Active responses were made with verbal prompt: scored '4'. He now seemed to wait for my cheering and smiled at once it was showered.

Session # 9

BASE LINE			INTERVENTION		
M3	Tongue Movement	3	M2	Blowing	3
C2	Give & Take	2	C1	Hello/Handshake	4
G1	Scribbling	2		-	

The usual 'Hello Aman' was accompanied by an extended hand. Unlike the previous days (when I took his hands in mine), 'my' hand was held up to him. He was held at the door and he wanted to come in. While the demand was persisted, I could see his hand rising. Then he was hesitant and held it back. As the demand was persistent, and monotonous, he complied and held my hands lightly saying 'allo'. Aman made an active response with the verbal prompt and was given a score of 4 for that. Reinforcement was contingently done.

He went directly to the trampoline, removed his shoes and jumped. When settled down to color, he made the usual unidirectional strokes: scored '2'.

When the candle was lit, I took his hands and made him 'feel the blow' softly. As the boy was reportedly sensitive to tactile stimulations small approximations were made. Aman peered interestingly. He was sensing the blow. The blow out gestures were made audible before blowing off the candle. As he was looking at my expressions, I puckered lips visibly, prompting him to do so. In response Aman blew out – a feeble one – but blown '**out**'. It was scored 3.

Give and take: Conversational interactions with children who have limited language skills should involve a short turn-taking format in which the adult and child alternately engage in actions with or without objects. It can be done following the child's lead in terms of interest or joint attention to objects and in a playful atmosphere, in which both adult and child are enjoying the time spent together. (Hagwood, 2009)

To observe 'Give and take' for shared play the observer was made to sit with Aman and the therapist sat across the room, on the floor. A toy car was pushed to Aman, which he promptly caught. When I asked, "**Give me**" he did not respond. Aman took the car eagerly, was observing its wheels, sniffed, and gave a quick lick. Then the observer physically prompted him to push it back to me and said "**give** the car back".His hands were stiff and was reluctant to hold the toy in order to push it back. When the grip was molded to grasp the car from the top and push it, a passive attempt was made. This was scored 2.

Tongue movement: This is a primitive, normal movement associated with the suckling pattern. The tongue extends between the teeth or gums. The tongue remains flat and thin with no abnormal tonal changes. (In the normal population, this may be called tongue thrust, especially by speech pathologists.) When asked show me your tongue, instead of tugging it out Aman opened his mouth wide and touched the tongue. Then he started playing with the spit.

'NO Aman it **stinks, don't do**' I said. He looked at me and continued the play. The saliva was wiped off. Aman when asked to tug out tongue after gently holding his hands, opened mouth and said 'ah'. The tongue was still, therefore scored 3 for the active attempt made with physical prompt.

Session # 10

BASE LINE		INTERVENTION	
M3 Tongue Movt	3	M2 Blowing	3
C2 Give & Take	3	C1 Hello/Handshake	4
G1 Scribbling	3	-	

I stood back from the door, extended hands and said "**Hello Aman**" when he walked in to the room. Aman walked up to me and held my hands! His response for the verbal prompt was scored 4. Associating the handshake to hello was still difficult. More prompts were required for that.

Tongue movement: Aman when asked to **tug out tongue** after gently holding his hands, opened mouth and said 'ah'. The tongue raised but not forward, therefore scored 3 for the active attempt made with physical prompt.

Scribbling now is continuous without lifting the pencil after a stroke. The efforts are passive yet done with verbal prompting, hence scored 3.

'*Give and take*' for shared play, after repeated prompting, he grabbed the car and attempted to respond. The observer helped him push it back. The active effort with physical prompting was scored 3.

Blowing: When the candle was lit, I took his hands and made him 'feel the blow' again. , I puckered my lips visibly prompting him to do it so. In response, Aman blew out feebly. He was scored 3 for the active attempt with physical prompt.

Session # 11

BASE LINE		INTERVENTION	
M3 Tongue movt	3	M2 Blowing	4
C2 Give & Take	3	C1 Hello/Handshake	4
G1 Scribbling	3	-	

A spontaneous greeting was never received from Aman but he started promptly responding to the Hello. Aman walked up to me and held my hands! His response for the verbal prompt was scored 4. When persisted, he said 'allo'.

Scribbling: When seated to scribbling he made continuous strokes. The efforts were passive, yet done with verbal prompting, hence scored 3.

Tongue movement: Aman when asked to tug out tongue, raised it but could not tug out, therefore, scored 3 for the active attempt made with physical prompt.

Give and take: After repeated prompting, he attempted to respond. Assistance was needed to push the car back. The active effort with physical prompting was scored 3.

Blowing – the therapist wanted to make him distinguish a soft blow and strong blow. The back of palm was held before the mouth and air was blown – first softly saying 'softly' and then strongly saying 'strongly.' Aman seemed grasping the idea properly. He could not perform it discretely but made a strong blowing on command and was scored 4.

Session # 12

BASE LINE			INTERVENTION	
M3 Tongue Movt	3	M2	Blowing	5
C2 Give & Take	3	C1	Hello/Handshake	4
G1 Scribbling	3		-	

For greeting, he said 'allo'. The response is quicker but he always waited for the verbal prompt; hence scored 4.

Aman when asked to tug out tongue raised it but could not tug out, therefore scored 3 for the active attempt made with physical prompt

For *Scribbling*, he made continuous strokes. The effort was passive yet done with verbal prompting, hence scored 3.

'Give and take' yielded stable score and response. The active effort with physical prompting was scored two.

Blowing: He blew off the candle immediately after I lit without a command. Aman was given the score 5 for the independent response.

Session # 13

BASE LINE			INTERVENTION	
M4 Gum movement	2	M3	Tongue Movt	4
C3 Imitates sequence	3	C2	Give & Take	4
G2 Dot to Dot joining	3	G1	Scribbling	3

Give and take: To teach him 'to give' edible reinforcers was used. As the toy is something children are reluctant to give, a more attractive bait was introduced - a lick of lollipop. Therapist sat with the kid and the observer sat across him. When she pushed the car to Aman saying, "Here Aman, catch it!" Aman caught it promptly – A loud cheering, clapping and a lick of lollipop were offered to him. He was so overwhelmed. "Now let's give it back and then lick the candy, OK?" He was so eager to have the sweet and quickly obliged. This time grasping was better! We pushed the car back – me holding his hands upon the car. Cheering was made again. He loved the play and the reinforcement served well. Aman was scored 4 for the active response with verbal prompt.

Tongue movement: Now the focus was shifted to tongue movement. Two candies (lollipops) were used. The therapist licked one candy holding it an inch away from mouth so that Aman could see the tongue reaching up to the candy. Aman when asked to **tug out tongue** could not do it. He kept his mouth open and was drooling profusely. He wanted to put the candy in his mouth. However, it was insisted to hold it outside and away from mouth. Aman was lured in between with its sweetness by giving a quick brushing on his lips so that the motivation does not wane. I could see his tongue reaching out slowly. Then the candy was held closer so that he could reach it. At times, he bent his head down to reach the sweet and I had to hold his head back.

With further attempts, he darted out his tongue once to take a lick and I could see tears rolling down the cheeks. Aman was given a warm hug and was let to put the candy in his mouth as a sign of recognition of his efforts. Verbalization of these has to be done continually no matter how he responds. His response was scored 4.

Scribbling: Music with uniform rhythm (rhymes) was played. Therapist sat as a model with a paper in front. Scribbling was done by the therapist with the rhythm of the rhyme. The child was gaping at the activity. The therapist sung along "old Mc Donald's" and did the scribbling in up, down, and circular movements. Then Aman was asked to join. He looked away. The therapist sat behind him held his hands and started the scribbling with music. After two trials, he made active attempts with physical prompt and was scored 3.

Dot to dot joining: The pre-writing activity was intended to develop stroke control and eye hand co-ordination. Two dots are made in his book. Aman was asked to **join them** and the therapist pointed to the dots. He seemed familiar with the task and made a stroke after several prompts without sustaining the eye contact. The location and dynamics of the stroke were appropriate but it did not touch the dots. The passive response with Verbal Prompts is scored 3.

Gum movement: Aman used to stiffen the body during feeding and also refused different textures of food (only pureed foods were eaten). He took long feeding times and had difficulty chewing. The occupational therapist suggested nutritional changes (food temperature and texture changes) postural or positioning changes (e.g., different seating) and behavior management techniques. The focus on intervention was to make the muscles of the mouth stronger by increasing tongue movement and improving chewing.

To check the baseline level a biscuit was given to Aman. He took it, sniffed and gave a lick. He started to suck when the therapist asked him to **bite it** and modeled biting through jaw movements. He did not make attempts at biting but the mandibles moved to shift the food, hence given a score of '2'.

Imitate sequence: The pre-intervention checklists indicated that Aman had problems in receptive listening and language, 'difficulty staying focused, over sensitivity to sounds'; and 'following only one or two instructions in sequence - hence the task was introduced.

Three gross motor movements were given to test the baseline. **'Aman! Do this – Wind up, pull and clap'**. He was familiar with the tasks but could not perform it in the sequence. Physical prompts were needed to continue the sequence, hence given the score 3.

Session # 14

BASE LINE		INTERVENTION	
M4 Gum movement	2	M3 Tongue movt	4
C3 Imitates sequence	3	C2 Give & Take	5
G2 Dot to Dot joining	3	G1 Scribbling	4

Give and take: When the car was pushed to Aman saying, "Here Aman, catch it!" Aman caught it promptly and pushed the car back to me holding his hands upon the car. He loved the play and the reinforcement helped. He was given a score of 5 for the spontaneous response.

Scribbling: Rhymes were played and therapist sat as the model for scribbling. Aman was asked to join. Initially his hand was held. The prompting was waned gradually and he scribbled continually. He started the scribbling without reluctance. Scored 4 for the response made on verbal prompt.

Tongue movement: For eliciting tongue movement, the therapist licked the candy holding it an inch away from mouth. Aman when asked to **tug out tongue** kept his mouth open; he was drooling profusely. With further prompting his tongue reached out and licked. He was given a score of 4.

Gum movement: He did not make attempts at biting but a passive effort was made to move the mandibles, hence given a score of '2'.

Imitate sequence: Three gross motor movements were given – **Wind up, pull and clap'**. He needed physical prompting to continue the sequence. Given the score 3.

Dot to dot joining: He made strokes after several prompts without sustaining the eye contact. The strokes do not touch the dots. The passive response with verbal prompts was scored 3.

Session # 15

BASE LINE		INTERVENTION	
M4 Gum movement	3	M3 Tongue movt	4
C3 Imitates sequence	4	C2 Give & Take	5
G2 Dot to Dot joining	4	G1 Scribbling	5

Give and take: When the car was pushed to Aman, he caught it promptly and pushed the car back to me holding his hands upon the car. Needed no prompting, hence scored 5.

Scribbling: Rhymes were played and he started scribbling with pencil without reluctance. Scored 5 for the independent response made.

Aman when asked to **tug out tongue** reached out his tongue to lick the candy. Scored 4.

Gum movement: He attempted at biting the biscuit, but the jaws never closed to bite. Hence given a score of 3.

Imitate sequence: **Wind up, pull and clap'**. He did the sequence with verbal prompt. Given the score 4.

Dot to dot joining: He made strokes after several prompts sustaining the eye contact and joined the dots. The response with verbal prompts was scored 4 but in most of the attempts his stroke went beyond the target, unnoticed.

Session # 16

No changes noticed from the previous session.

Session # 17

BASE LINE		INTERVENTION	
M5 Sipping	1	M4 Gum movement	4
C4 Response to call	2	C3 Imitates sequence	5
G3 Peg board	3	G2 Dot to Dot joining	4

Peg Board: In order to check the fine motor co ordination skill a Designer Peg Board was used (Figure 6). Fine motor coordination involved the ability to control the small muscles of the hand and fingers to perform precise manipulative movements. The board consisted of a thick plastic rectangular mat (15cm x10 cm) and a pack of sphere headed plastic nails (1.5 cm long and 1cm diameter for the bob as shown in Figure 6). The instruction was **"Aman, try to put these pegs into the mat"**. The multicolored pegs attract children and immediately grabbed a handful of pegs. No further eye contact was maintained by Aman. He took one peg and fondled it for a long time when the therapist asked him to place it on the board. After much coaxing despite his passive efforts, four of them were placed. Therefore, he was given a score of 3.

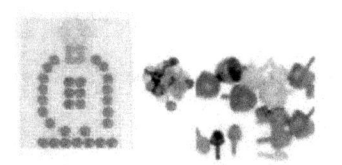

Figure 6. Assistive device used - Designer Pegboard

Response to call: Aman's mother complained that he lacked a consistent response to name call. The baseline included observing the child's ability to orient socially when called by his name. In the school also Aman usually does not respond to his name being called. When it is repeated, or for an alarming call, sometimes he looks, but not consistently. He makes a brief eye contact even when tapped on the shoulder. The passive response with physical prompting is scored 2.

Sipping: It was noticed Aman did not like to sip from a glass, by pressing his lip on hard glass. The milk was poured into the glass (not up to the brim) and offered to him. Aman wanted it to be poured into his mouth and gulped, but he was not let to do so. The task was scored 1 as he turned away his face.

Gum movement: A chewy tube (an oral motor tool) was inserted into Aman's mouth. The tube is held on the mandibular molar teeth (teeth distal from midline on the lower jaw). It was seen that Aman was biting the tube softly when asked to chew. Aman was given a score of 4.

Imitate sequence: A rhyme is sung with the three moves in a sequence.

' Wind up, Wind the bobbin, Wind up, Wind the bobbin

Pull, pull, clap, clap, clap'. He did the sequence with verbal prompt. On later trials he was so eager to perform and made the movements without the prompt, hence given the score 5.

Dot to dot joining: On the board, several pairs of dots were marked (Figure 7) and the therapist held Aman's hand to model. Aman was told, **"You have to join the dots, i.e from here to here. Like this, 'go down and stop'!"** After several strokes the prompts were waned, Aman sustained eye contact and joined the dots. Still he needed the stop signal to locate the end. The response with verbal prompts was scored 4.

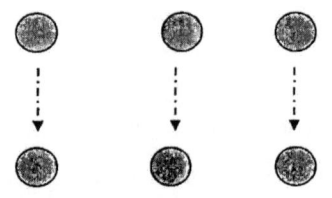

Figure 7 Dot to dot joining tasks

Session #18

BASE LINE		INTERVENTION	
M5 Sipping	1	M4 Gum movement	3
C4 Response to call	2	C3 Imitates sequence	5
G3 Peg board	3	G2 Dot to Dot joining	4

Gum movement: He did not chew when the tube was removed from the mouth. He tried to suck on the biscuit, which was not allowed. I made a spontaneous "Tch" (exclamation used to express irritation, annoyance, or impatience) he did not like this and started the whimpering. In the later trials, he made passive response with verbal prompting. This was scored 3.

Imitate sequence: when the rhyme was sung he started winding movements, then hesitated with the next move. With further trials, he made the moves in a sequence. He was given the score 5.

Dot to dot joining: The dots were presented without the prompt. He looked at me expecting the aid. When no signs of help were given, he started extending his elbow so that it is held to draw! So the verbal prompt was reinstated. Score 4.

Sipping: Aman could not sip from the glass. He tried to tug out his tongue to lick up the milk. His head bowed down to reach the glass, which was held back gently by the therapist. The task is scored 1.

Response to call: Aman makes the same passive response to physical prompting. So is scored 2.

Peg Board: In order to improve the fine motor co ordination, eye contact was needed which was not maintained consistently by Aman. He fondled the pegs for a long time and needed coaxing to place it on the board. Therefore he was given a score of 3.

Session #19

BASE LINE		INTERVENTION	
M5 Sipping	1	M4 Gum movement	4
C4 Response to call	2	C3 Imitates sequence	3
G3 Peg board	3	G2 Dot to Dot joining	4

Sipping: Aman could not sip from the glass. He got irritated when he could not reach the milk and broke down to tears. It took much effort to soothe him down and so he started rejecting when the next task was introduced, i.e., imitating sequence. The sipping was scored 1.

Response to call: Aman was not at all aroused by the name call. He looked up at times. So, was scored 2.

Peg Board: Still needed coaxing to place it on the board. Therefore, given a score of 3.

Imitate sequence: After giving other tasks, when the rhyme was resumed, he started the movements reluctantly. With further prompted trials, he made the moves in a sequence. He was given the score 3.

Dot to dot joining: The dots were presented without the prompt. He looked at me without drawing. Needed persistent attempts at improving the execution of task without help. Hence the verbal prompt was reinstated. Score 4.

Gum movement: He was let to chew the tube, then the biscuit was introduced with the command "Aman I want you to bite this like this", and the therapist crunched one biscuit noisily so that the kid noticed the biscuit grinding in between the therapist's teeth. He tried to bite on the biscuit, which was a feeble soft attempt. Later, the response was elicited with verbal prompting and was scored 4.

Session #20

BASE LINE		INTERVENTION	
M5 Sipping	1	M4 Gum movement	4
C4 Response to call	2	C3 Imitates sequence	4
G3 Peg board	3	G2 Dot to Dot joining	5

Activities showed a stable score. Sequence imitating was better for which only the verbal prompting was needed.

Session # 21

BASE LINE		INTERVENTION	
M6 Deep breathing	2	M5 Sipping	3
C5 Identify familiar person	3	C4 Response to call	4
G4 Draw in 4 directions	3	G3 Peg board	4

Peg Board: The bowl of pins was kept on the left side of the table and the mat was kept on the right side. Aman was asked to pick up the peg-using left hand and pass it on to the right hand. The right hand was gently held so that he used his left hand for picking up. He had to pay some attention to do this. Then he was made to insert it into the mat. The intention was to make him sense the peg with fingers for a few more seconds. Eventually he started paying some eye contact to the thing – manipulated it with fingers, turned its bob up, held on it and pushed it down into the mat. All the while, the therapist gave verbal prompts and cheers to the child to keep up his efforts. He was scored 4.

Sipping: -The glass was held outside his teeth margin and tilted to his mouth (as in Figure 8). He was asked to close the lips and drink. Aman tried to tug out his tongue to lick up the milk. His head bowed to reach the glass, which was held back by the therapist, as the intention was to make him pucker his lips and close at the brim of the glass. The therapist modeled sipping with a transparent glass of water. Aman was desperate and I could see his lips puckering to take in the milk. At that moment the glass was tilted more towards him so that the milk was reachable. Aman breathed in orally and reached the milk meanwhile closing the lips at the brim of glass. Loud applause was given and Aman seemed so happy. The active attempt with physical prompting was scored 3.

Figure 8 Assistive technique - Sipping

Response to call: Aman was held close and rocked. His name was called in rhythm with the rocking and the therapist herself made a humming as a response. (The response chosen was the sound he could elicit) Aman seemed enjoying the rocking and was listening as well. After so many trials, the name was called and the rocking was stopped abruptly. I could feel Aman pushing me to continue the rocking, and then he was prompted to hum. Still lot of attempts were needed to make it a habit, calling him and he giving the response in tempo. Scored 4 for the best response.

Deep breathing: Taking deep breaths and holding poses can help reduce outside distractions and calm children. Aman is asked to breathe in and out. Therapist modeled for him. Aman needed persistent attempts to look at what I was doing. Finally, he did a chin up – down motion. The response was scored 2.

Identify familiar person: The task is in the Curriculum Guide for Autistic children (Maurice, 1996). The teachers reported that they have tried to make him point to familiar people and they were not successful in the attempt. Therefore, a task was designed to check whether he identified familiar people. Aman was asked to hand over a pencil box to Manu yet another kid in the classroom. Both of them had been in the same classroom for the past two and half years. Therefore, it was assumed that they are familiar with each other. However, a response towards a familiar person was not observed (as reported by the teachers) from Aman. With physical prompting, he handed over the box to Manu. A score of 3 was given.

Draw in four directions: The goal was to check his sense towards directions of the strokes, which invariably affects the dynamics of writing. **Aman draw 'down'** was said and the therapist modeled it on a paper. Aman made a stroke down. However, for the further directional commands also he drew in the same direction (for Up, forward and backward). With physical prompts, he drew in the four directions but seldom repeated. Hence, given a score 3.

Session # 22

BASE LINE		INTERVENTION	
M6 Deep breathing	2	M5 Sipping	4
C5 Identify familiar person	3	C4 Response to call	4
G4 Draw in 4 directions	3	G3 Peg board	4

Peg Board: Aman picked up the peg-using left hand and passed it on to the right hand. He paid attention and inserted it into the mat. The therapist had to give verbal prompts and cheers to the child to keep up his efforts. When the prompting waned, his eye contact was lost; hence it had to be reinstated. He was scored 4.

Sipping: Aman's lips puckered to take in the milk. Later he did it with verbal prompts. The glass is tilted more towards him so that the milk was reachable. Aman attempts to close the lips at the brim of glass. Loud applause was given as for Aman it was a difficult task. The active attempt with verbal prompting was scored 4.

Response to call: Aman liked being rocked. As done in the previous session after so many trials, the name was called and the rocking was stopped abruptly. I could feel Aman pushing me to continue the rocking, and then he was prompted to say /o/. Promptly he started giving the response in response to the name call. Again scored 4 for the best response.

Deep breathing: Aman was asked to breathe in and out. Therapist modeled for him. Aman looked away most of the time, when insisted, did an up – down motion with head mimicking me. The response was scored 2.

Identify familiar person: Aman was asked to hand over a box to Manu. He needed physical prompting, to perform the task. A score of 3 was given.

Draw in four directions: Aman made unidirectional strokes -- downwards only. With physical prompts, he drew in all directions. Hence, given a score 3.

Session # 23

BASE LINE		INTERVENTION	
M6 Deep breathing	3	M5 Sipping	4
C5 Identify familiar person	3	C4 Response to call	4
G4 draw in 4 directions	3	G3 Peg board	4

All the task scores remained stable as the previous session except breathing tasks.

Deep breathing: Aman mimicked the head movement of the therapist doing breathe in and out. He was seen breathing out with the nodding of head and was scored 3.

Session # 24

BASE LINE		INTERVENTION	
M6 Deep breathing	3	M5 Sipping	5
C5 Identify familiar person	3	C4 Response to call	4
G4 draw in 4 directions	3	G3 Peg board	5

Sipping: Aman sipped the milk from the glass. He did not wait for the commands. Scored 5 for the spontaneous response.

Peg Board: Aman picked up the peg-using left hand and passed it on to the right hand. He inserted it into the mat. The therapist did not have to prompt. He was driven by the success of the previous task - sipping -and hence performed better. Scored 5 for the Independent response.

All the other task scores remained consistent as the previous session.

Session # 25

BASE LINE		INTERVENTION	
M7 Descend one step per tread	1	M6 Deep breathing	4
C6 possession 'whose'	2	C5 Identify familiar person	4
G5 draw a shape	3	G4 draw in 4 directions	3

Deep breathing: It was noticed that Aman breathed out saying /ha/ mimicking the therapist. Now the therapist modelled with hand movements also – waving up for inhalation and waving down for exhalation in rhythm. The / ha / sound was also made for exhalation. As Aman took short breaths, the hand stopped halfway indicating it should prolong. With further attempts, the breaths were taken with verbal prompts hence it was given a score of 4.

Identify familiar person: Aman was made to touch Manu with the left hand, while he had the box on the right. Verbal prompting was given as affirmations, "Yes, that is Manu. Give the box to Manu". He needed physical prompting initially. As the trials progressed, we could make him pass the box to Manu without physical prompts. A score of 4 was given.

Draw in four directions:

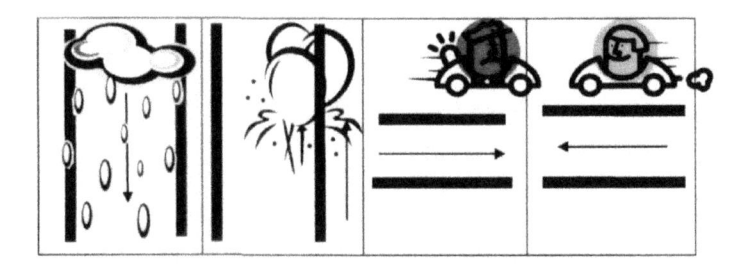

Figure 9 Assistive technique for drawing in four directions

Aman was given thick stripes as margins (Figure 9) within which he was made to draw, along with the therapist, continually - saying

'Down, down - the rain comes down' (For downward stroke)

Balloon goes up, up, up (For upward stroke)

Car goes forward (For forward stroke)

It goes back too! (For backward stroke). He drew well in one direction a time but kept on hanging back for 'hand on hand' support. Aman was scored 3.

Descend one-step per tread: Aman lacked refined walking and running skills. The child was not able to climb and descend stairs with alternating feet and run on toes.

Aman was asked to **step down from a stair.** He took steps one by one. He was given the score 1. On further attempts, he was asked to step down continually with alternating feet. Still he did not seem to comprehend the command.

Whose? - Possession: Whose indicates possession, and like which and what, could be used with or without a noun as a question word. The therapist showed palm and asked, "Whose hand, Aman?" He nodded and touched himself, his hand and then mine. Aman made some responses, but illogical. He was physically prompted to touch me as the person whose hand was being shown. He was given a score of 2 as he made passive attempts with physical prompting.

Draw a shape: Triangle. Aman was making strokes in stipulated directions, hence drawing a shape was chosen as the goal. Three dots were drawn on a paper and he was asked to **join them to form a Triangle.** He needed physical prompting to join the dots continually. He had the tendency to stop at a dot and skip to the next one but connecting it with a line was difficult. After lot of physical prompting, he did and was scored 3.

Session # 26

BASE LINE		INTERVENTION	
M7 Descend one step per tread	1	M6 Deep breathing	4
C6 possession 'whose'	2	C5 Identify familiar person	4
G5 draw a shape	3	G4 draw in 4 directions	4

Draw in four directions: Aman could easily follow the verbal prompts and draw in the corresponding page showing direction. Therefore a score of 4 was given.

For the rest of the activities the scores remained stable as the previous day.

Session # 27

BASE LINE		INTERVENTION	
M7 Descend one step per tread	1	M6 Deep breathing	4
C6 possession 'whose'	2	C5 Identify familiar person	4
G5 draw a shape	3	G4 draw in 4 directions	5

Deep breathing: Aman breathed out saying /ha/ mimicking the therapist's hand movements. When the hand stopped on the way, he did it again. With further attempts, the breath was taken with verbal prompts. Therefore a score of 4 was given.

Identify familiar person: Aman touched Manu with the left hand, when he had the box on the right. verbal prompting was given as affirmations, "Yes, that is Manu. Give the box to Manu". A score of 4 was given.

Draw in four directions: Aman drew in the four directions when given the particular page (With visual aid). The task was performed independently, hence scored 5.

Descend one-step per tread: Aman still took steps one by one. He was given the score one.

Possession: when the therapist showed her palm and asked, "Whose hand is this, Aman?" He touched himself first, and then the therapists hand. He was given a score of 2.

Draw a shape: Triangle. Aman needed physical prompting to join the dots continually. He had the tendency to stop at a dot and skip to the next one but connecting it with a line was difficult. After lot of physical prompting, he did it. Therefore, he was scored 3.

Session # 28

BASE LINE		INTERVENTION	
M7 Descend one step per tread	1	M6 Deep breathing	4
C6 possession 'whose'	2	C5 Identify familiar person	4
G5 draw a shape	3	G4 draw in 4 directions	5

All tasks showed stable scores as the previous session.

Session # 29

BASE LINE		INTERVENTION	
		M7 Descend one step per tread	3
C7 Yes / No gesture	1	C6 possession 'whose'	3
G6 Picture Identification	3	G5 draw a shape	4

Descend one-step per tread: The therapist crouched in front of the kid and touched his calf alternately. Aman forwarded the corresponding leg supporting himself on the railing. Verbal prompting was also given to **step down, one - two - one - two**. On further trials, the corresponding leg was touched using a long scale. If he joined both legs on a step the physical prompting was reinstated. Aman was given 3 points for active response with physical prompting.

Possession: The therapist made palm print on Aman's book and then his' on the adjacent page with color. Aman noticed either page. He was told, "Miss's hand (pointing to the print) and this one? - Aman's". The contiguous pairing of touching of the page and then to a person continued several times. When his palm was pressed firmly to me, it was noticed that he no longer curled his fingers. The task was intended for creating an association between the pictures to person who possessed that. However, he still needed the physical prompting to make the appropriate response. Aman made active responses with physical prompts; therefore a score of 3 was given.

Draw a shape: Triangle. Aman needed physical prompting to join the dots continually. Three dots were then drawn on a vertical board. The therapist made him hold the pencil and drew continually saying "one‖ two‖ three ‖ **AGAIN** one ‖ two ‖ three ‖ **TRIANGLE**". This repeated several times – I could sense his grip gaining momentum with the rhythm. Now the physical prompting was waned and I could see him drawing from one dot to the other completing a triangle but he would stop if the verbal prompting stopped. Aman was given 4 points for active response with verbal prompting.

Yes / No gesture: Aman did not make gestures as reported by the parents and special educators.. Aman had a liking for the trampoline. Therefore, he was asked "Aman Jump on the trampoline?" He immediately got up and started pulling me to go to the trampoline, (which was now placed in the play therapy room). "Aman you should say 'yes'" - I would nod my head for 'yes' and shake my head for 'no' when asking him if he wanted something. However, he would not use the gestures for expression. He still pulled me. Aman was given a score of 1 for not making a gesture for 'Yes'. In this task, there arose no chance for 'No'.

Picture Identification: Attributes such as object or picture familiarity (Lachman & Lachman, 1980) are known to correlate well with cognitive measures, and affect both memory and retrieval processes. The task was one, which the parents as well as the special educator reported that he does not perform.

Pictorial aid (of bags) were placed on the table (Figure 10) and the boy was told 'Aman see this? This one is Sam's Bag' (the middle one). He looked away. On further trials, he was made to touch the picture of Sam's bag and prompted to pick. Aman was given a score of three for the active response with physical prompting. The task was designed so because the teachers have noticed that the child had a liking towards the picture on Sam's bag.

Figure 10 - Pictorial aid for "whose?"

Session # 30

BASE LINE		INTERVENTION	
		M7 Descend one step per tread	3
C7 Yes / No gesture	1	C6 possession 'whose'	4
G6 Picture Identification	3	G5 draw a shape	4

Descend one-step per tread: Aman made active responses with physical prompts; therefore a score of three was given.

Possession: The contiguous pairing of the touching of the page to a person helped creating an association. When asked, "Whose hand?"- By showing my palm print, he tapped on my shoulder. Before he could make it his illogical string of response, by touching him and me alternately, I cheered aloud 'yes!! This is miss's hand... and whose is this?' – By touching his palm print. Aman responded appropriately. He was given a score of four. This was repeated to strengthen the S-R connection.

Draw a shape: Triangle. When verbally prompted Aman drew from one dot to the other completing a triangle. Aman was given 4 points for active response with verbal prompting..

Yes / No gesture: Aman was given one point for not making a gesture for 'Yes'. He does not have the habit of that fragment of communication.

Picture Identification: The three pictures were placed on the table and Aman was asked to pick up Sam's bag. He looked away. Again, he was made to touch the appropriate picture and he picked it up. Aman was given a score of three for the active response with physical prompting.

Session # 31

BASE LINE		INTERVENTION	
		M7 Descend one step per tread	3
C7 Yes / No gesture	1	C6 possession 'whose'	5
G6 Picture Identification	3	G5 draw a shape	4

Descend one-step per tread: Aman needed physical prompting but the kid was actively involved. Therefore, he was given a score of three.

Possession: Aman touched the page and touched me back when my palm print was shown and so with his'. Aman was given five points for the spontaneous response.

Draw a shape: Triangle. When verbally prompted Aman drew from one dot to the other completing a triangle. Aman was given 3 points for active response with physical prompting.

Yes / No gesture: Aman did not make the gesture in the expected format and was scored one.

Picture Identification: Aman was asked to pick up picture of Sam's bag. Aman was given a score of three for picking it up with physical prompting.

Session # 32

BASE LINE		INTERVENTION	
		M7 Descend one step per tread	4
C7 Yes / No gesture	1	C6 possession 'whose'	5
G6 Picture Identification	3	G5 draw a shape	4

Descend one-step per tread: Aman Descended one-step per tread with verbal prompting alone. He was given 4 points.

Possession: Aman spontaneously touched the page and touched me back when my palm print was shown and so with his' and it was also noticed that he was distinguishing the two prints well. He was given 5 points for that.

All the other activity (baseline and intervention) scores remained stable.

<u>Session # 33</u>

BASE LINE		INTERVENTION	
		C7 Yes / No gesture	2
G7 Writing an alphabet	3	G6 Picture Identification	3

Yes / No gesture: Aman was seated at eyelevel and told "I want you to say yes" and I nodded my head along with. So tell me **you want to go for jumping?** I nodded wide-eyed saying an emphatic **yes**. Aman got restless and pulled me even more."No Aman, not like that, Say **YES**" I nodded – repeating the Yes several times. I held his head and helped him nod. He co-operated fast, as he was eager to go for Jumping. Given a score of 2 for the effort made with physical prompting.

Picture Identification: Sam's bag was brought to the room. Aman was shown the bag and the photo with an exaggerated tone,"Hey you see this Aman?" The bag was put on his lap and the photo was kept in front, Aman was made to look at the two and see that they were the same. Now he was asked to pick Sam's bag from the three. Still he was slow to pick the picture and was given a score of 3 for picking with physical prompting. Aman was busy watching the bag closely. In the class the bags were kept in a rack and the kids were not allowed to handle one other's things.

Writing an alphabet: Aman knew how to draw strokes and circle, hence it was planned to introduce the letter L: a straight-line letter with strokes in two directions – down and forward. Dots were put in the book for connecting to form L.

Aman made active attempts with physical prompting, hence scored 3.

<u>Session # 34</u>

BASE LINE		INTERVENTION	
G7 Writing an alphabet	3	C7 Yes / No gesture	3
		G6 Picture Identification	4

Yes / No gesture: Aman loved trampoline, so he readily mimiced the nodding. Now with the verbal prompt he showed the gesture and sprinted to the playroom. Given 3 points for the response.

Picture Identification: Sam's bag was kept on the table. Now Aman looked at the bag and picks the photo, but hesitated to get the affirmative prompt from me given a score of 4 for picking with verbal prompting.

Writing an alphabet: Dots were put in the book for connecting to form L. Aman needed physical prompting to write, hence scored three.

<u>Session # 35</u>

BASE LINE		INTERVENTION	
G7 Writing an alphabet	3	C7 Yes / No gesture	2
		G6 Picture Identification	4

The session was resumed after five days as the kid was down with fever.

Yes / No gesture: Aman was not responding eagerly. He still had running nose and the scores of the tasks declined. I rephrased the stimuli as "would you like to go jumping?" "Dear, you should say Yes (nodding) if you want to". I held his head and facilitated a slow nod. Given 2 points for the response.

Picture Identification: I gave the affirmative verbal prompt and he touched the correct picture with no difficulty. He was given a score of 4 for picking with verbal prompting.

Writing an alphabet: Aman was given physical prompting to write, hence scored 3.

Session # 36

BASE LINE		INTERVENTION	
G7 Writing an alphabet	3	C7 Yes / No gesture	3
		G6 Picture Identification	4

Yes / No gesture: Aman made an awkward nod in order to get to trampoline. The passive attempt with verbal prompting was given 3 points.

Picture Identification: He touched the correct picture with no difficulty. He was given a score of 4 points for picking with verbal prompting.

Writing an alphabet: Aman waited for physical prompting to write, hence scored 3.

Session # 37

BASE LINE	INTERVENTION	
	G7 Writing an alphabet	3

Writing an alphabet: Aman was told," **Go down and forward**" (in vernacular). The therapist modeled the direction on yet another sheet by holding his hand. Since physical prompting was needed to write, scored three. Figure 11 shows the aid given.

Figure 11. Writing Aid

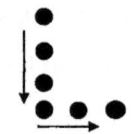

Table 3. The Scores for response strength of first participant

Legend: B- Baseline, I- Intervention

Activity /Session		1	2	3	4	5	6	7	8	9	10	11	12	13	14	15	16	17	18	19	20	21	22	23	24	25	26	27	28	29	30	31	32	33	34	35	36	37	38	39	40
M1	Jumping	1	1	1	1	2	3	3	4	4	4	4	4																												
C1	Hello/Handshake	2	2	2	2	2	2	2	2	4	4	4	3	3	4	5	5																								
G1	Scribbling	2	2	2	2	2	2	2	2	3	3	3	3	3	4	5	5																								
M2	Blowing					1	2	2	2	3	3	4	5																												
C2	Give & take									2	3	3	3	4	5	5	5																								
G2	Dot to dot												3	3	3	4	4	4	4	4	5																				
M3	Tongue movt.									3	3	3	3	4	4	4																									
C3	Action chain													3	3	4	4	5	5	3	4	4	4	4	5																
G3	Peg board																	3	3	3	3	3	4	4	4	4	4	4	3	4	4	5	3								
M4	Gum movt.																	4	3	4	4	3	3	3	5	3	3	3													
C4	Respond to call													2	2	3	3	2	2	2	2																				
G4	Draw in 4 dirn.																	2	2	2		3	3	3	3	3	4	4	3	4	4	5	5								
M5	Sipping																		1	1	1	3	3	3	5	3	4	5					3								
C5	Identify people																					3	3	3	3	4	4	4	4	4	4	4	3								
G5	Draw shapes																									4	3	3	3	3	4	5	5								
M6	Deep breathe																					2	2			4	4	4	3	4	5	3	3								
C6	Whose?																									2	2	2	2	3	4	5	4								
G6	Picture Idntfctn																									2	2	2	2	3	3	3	3	3	4	4	4				
M7	Descend																									1	1	1	1	1	1	1	1								
C7	Yes/ No gesture																													3	3	3	3	2	3	2	3	3			
G7	Writing																													3	3	3	3	3	3	3	3	3	4	4	4

Session # 38

BASE LINE	INTERVENTION	
	G7 Writing an alphabet	4

Writing an alphabet: Aman was given verbal prompting to write **down and forward**, and he could make it, therefore scored four.

Session # 39

BASE LINE	INTERVENTION	
	G7 Writing an alphabet	4

Session # 40

BASE LINE	INTERVENTION	
	G7 Writing an alphabet	4

Aman scored stable for the two sessions.

The scores for response strength of First Participant – Aman over the three month period is condensed and listed in Table 3.

3.4.3.2. Participant 2 - SAM

Intervention plan

The intervention plan for three months for the second participant is shown in Table 4.

Session # 1

	BASE LINE		INTERVENTION
M1	Give and take	2	
C1	Eye contact	1	
G1	Scribbling	2	

Sam clinged to the caretaker and was reluctant to come into the room. He held a downward gaze and was whimpering when brought to the seat. He did not look in my direction,

Table 4 Intervention plan for the second participant for three months

Activity /Session No		1	2	3	4	5	6	7	8	9	10	11	12	13	14	15	16	17	18	19	20	21	22	23	24	25	26	27	28	29	30	31	32	33	34
M1	Give & take	B	B	B	B	B	B	B																											
C1	Eye contact	B	B	B	B	B	B	B	B	I	I	I	I	I	I	I																			
G1	Scribbling	B	B	B	B	B	B	B	B	B	B	B	B	I	I	I	I	I	I																
M2	Pick & drop					B	B	B	B																										
C2	Hello/ Handshke									B	B	B	B	I	I	I	I	I	I																
G2	Rolling dough													I		I	I	I	I	I	I	I	I												
M3	Jumping									B	B	B	B	B	B	B	B	I	I	I	I	I	I												
C3	Oral-motormovt.													I	I	I	I	I	I	B	B	I	I	I	I	I	I								
G3	Object Idntfction													B	B	B	B	I	B	B	B	B	B	B	B	I	I								
M4 Texture sensing														B	B	B	B																		
C4 Body part																				B	I	B			I	I	I	I	I	I	I				
G4	Peg board																			B	B	B	B	B	B	I	I	I	I	I	I				
M5	Sipping																			B	B	B	I	I	I	I	I	I	I	I					
C5	High five																			B	B	B	B	B	B	I	I	I	I	I	I	I	I	I	
G5	Coloring																									B	B	B	B	I	I	I	I	I	I

B- Baseline
I- Intervention

though he was aware of my presence. In order to seek his attention, I brought sound and light emitting toys, which usually fascinate kids.

Give and take: A car was pushed to Sam saying "**hey Sam! You like this? Take it!** " His face expressed nothing but he touched the car, which came and stopped before him. Sam took the big car, moved it back and forth on the floor, and peered at the rotating wheels. The therapist asked,

"**Give me**".

Would you give it back to me?

Sam can I have the car back?"

The observer held his hand and pushed back the car saying, "**give the car back**". Sam let his hand to be held and observed the car being pushed back. He was given a score of 2 as it was a passive attempt with physical prompt.

Making eye contact: Eye contact was never maintained and every attempt done was deliberately avoided by the child. Even a spontaneous alarming call did not elicit a response from him. He was given a score of 1.

Scribbling: According to Crosser (2008) the act of scribbling can serve several useful purposes for the young child. Small muscle coordination and control improve with practice, cognitive abilities are exercised, opportunities for social interaction arise, and the physical movements provide emotional release. As a toddler's small muscle control is not fully developed, he or she may approach the drawing task by grasping the marker with his or her fist, creating a bit of difficulty placing the marks exactly where he or she wants them. Movements were typically large, involving the entire arm with little finger or wrist control. This is because the pattern of physical development proceeds from the center of the trunk outward. A rhythmic, repetitive, scrubbing motion is common among children, providing sensory enjoyment and making drawing a very physical act.

Crayons were assorted on the table to see whether he was familiar with them. When he did not seem paying attention, the therapist asked, "**Shall we color?** After multiple persuasions, he picked up a crayon and made strokes on the table. He was given a score of 2.

The whole session was very mechanical. He got up and left eagerly.

Session # 2

	BASE LINE		INTERVENTION
M1	Give and take	2	
C1	Eye contact	1	
G1	Scribbling	3	

Sam seemed the difficult to impress type. Sam was not at all expressive. The second day also went the same way.

Give and take: He pushed the car with disinterest. He was scored two.

Eye contact was minimal; he was given a score of one.

Scribbling: He took the crayon after much physical prompts and made a circular scribbling on the paper. He was given a score of 3.

Session # 3

	BASE LINE		INTERVENTION
M1	Give and take	1	
C1	Eye contact	2	
G1	Scribbling	3	

Sam came in irritated. The caretaker mentioned that he had an uncleared bowel for two days. The boy was gritting his teeth and hitting his head (mild tapping) intermittently. I held him close and said" its ok, just tell me if your tummy hurts. Ok dear!" He immediately looked at me. The physical prompt and the reassurance must have made him look at me at that instant. He was given a score of two.

Give and take: He did not care about the car even though persistent attempts were made. In between, he looked at me as if searching something. I could not decipher the meaning of the scanning he made. He was scored one for the blank response.

Scribbling: Sam made a curl with physical prompting but it was an active effort. He was given a score of three.

Session # 4

	BASE LINE		INTERVENTION
M1	Give and take	2	
C1	Eye contact	2	
G1	Scribbling	3	

Sam came in giggling when the caretaker ruffled his hair. He was reported as having a cleared bowel. He did not look when I greeted him.

Give and take: He pushed the car with no direction when the observer held his hand. However, the push was given a score of 2.

Eye contact: when he was held close and prompted saying, "Sam look here" he swiped his eyes. It was passive – in search of something. He was given a score of 2.

Scribbling: Curls were drawn with physical prompting. I could feel his tripod grip on the crayon-getting firm. He was scored 3.

Session # 5

	BASE LINE			INTERVENTION	
M2	Pick and drop	1	M1	Give and take	3
C1	Eye contact	2			
G1	Scribbling	3			

Give and take: The observer pushed the car towards Sam with the same command "Hey, take it". I sat on the floor with him and cheered when he caught the car mid way. A tight hug was given which made him smile. Deep touch pressure is the type of surface pressure that is exerted in most types of firm touching. It has been found to have beneficial effects in a variety of clinical settings (Ayres, 1979). In anecdotal reports, deep touch pressure has been described to produce a calming effect in children. He was prompted to hold the car firmly and to push it back. I could notice him leaning on to me and gaining interest in the task. The active attempt was scored 3.

Eye contact was still a flutter of eyelids in my direction when repeatedly called for attention. The prompted response was scored 2.

Scribbling still needs physical prompting but he performed it. The score was 3.

Pick and drop: Following two step directions is achieved normally within three years (REELS, 1971). A bowl of colorful beads (one-inch size) was held up to Sam (Figure 12). He was asked to **pick a bead and drop it into the bowl** kept next to him on the table itself. The bowl was kept towards the left side on the table and the bowl into which 'to be dropped' towards the right side.

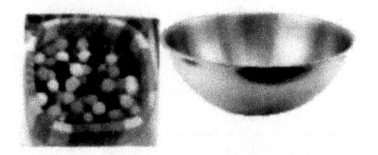

Figure 12 Assistive Device - pick and drop

Crossing the midline is the ability to reach with the right hand or leg over the midline to the left side of the body, not moving the body, and twisting toward one side. Having efficient bilateral coordination enables both feet or both hands to work together. This allows to play and work with fluid body movements. Bilateral coordination and crossing the body's midline also support a child's development of fine motor skills, ability to use tools, and ability to visually track a moving object. Deficits in bilateral integration were linked with deficits in sequencing (Ayres, 1989).

Even after physical prompts Sam did not care to grab a bead at least. He was scored one for the blank response.

Session # 6

	BASE LINE			INTERVENTION	
M2	Pick and drop	1	M1	Give and take	3
C1	Eye contact	2			
G1	Scribbling	3			

The activities did not show a hike or drop in scoring on this day. While pushing the car Sam was continually asked to hold it firmly - as I could feel his palm too flaccid, even though he was gaining interest in the task. The active attempt with physical prompt is given a score of 3.

Session # 7

	BASE LINE			INTERVENTION	
M2	Pick and drop	1	M1	Give and take	5
C1	Eye contact	2			
G1	Scribbling	3			

Pick and drop: Sam was so immobile on some days. He would sit back staring into space even when he was continually prompted. He pulled back his hands and looked away when the bowl of beads was held closer. He was given a score of 1.

Eye contact: Scored 2 for the passive response he made with much prompting.

Scribbling: Scored three for the active attempt with physical prompt.

Give and take: Sam now could catch the car when the observer pushed it towards him. We would cheer and clap following this response. He did not look at me though I could feel him sitting closer enough for some reassurance. It was noticed that holding him firmly helped communication better. Therefore, when the car was being pushed I receded the support given to Sam's right hand, which pushed the car, firmly gripped the left shoulder, and verbally prompted to push the car back to the observer. This worked and Sam pushed the car back. We cheered and he was scored 5.

Session # 8

	BASE LINE			INTERVENTION	
M2	Pick and drop	1	M1	Give and take	3
C1	Eye contact	2			
G1	Scribbling	3			

The baseline assessment activities did not show any variation from the previous session.

Give and take: That day when I receded the support he caught my hand and made me hold his' in order to push the car back to the observer. However, he seemed to have grasped the idea of give and take. The active attempt with physical prompt was scored 3.

Session # 9

	BASE LINE			INTERVENTION	
M3	Jumping	1	M1	Give and take	3
			M2	Pick and drop	2
C2	Hello/Handshake	1	C1	Eye contact	4
G1	Scribbling	3			

Hello/Handshake: When brought to the room a warm greeting was given as "Hello Sam!" His head turned to the direction of the hail but he did not make any eye contact. No willful attempts were made to communicate either. I grasped his hands, which do not even mould to grasp mine. Hence a score of 1 was given.

Jumping: In order to find out the baseline level performance the child was asked "Sam how do you **jump**?

"**Would you Jump for me?**" He did not respond. He was scored 1.

Scribbling: Sam does scribbling with physical prompting; therefore, he was given a score of 3.

Give and take: Sam now catches the car when said, "Take it Sam". However, to give it back he needed physical prompting. He was given a score of 3 points.

Pick and drop: The bead was picked saying **'PICK'** and dropped into the metal bowl saying 'and **DROP'**. The procedure was repeated monotonously for at least 10 times so that the child could sense the sound of me picking a bead and then dropping it to the metal bowl in a rhythm. Afterwards his hand was also led into the bowl of beads very passively all the while I continued the Pick and Drop process. When it was noticed he had a flaccid grip on the beads physical prompt was given. He grasped one bead but to drop it into the metal bowl several verbal prompts and physical prompting was needed. He could not let the bead go off his grip. He were given a score of 2.

Eye contact: to enhance eye contact Sam was seated at eyelevel with me. I had to hold him close, touch his cheeks and call repeatedly to get an evasive look from him! I tried verbalizing the need. "Sam I want you to look at me when I talk to you ok!" The persuasion was gentle and warm but loud enough to catch a glaring from him. My eyes smiled to meet his'. He looked away immediately but was given a score of 4, as he made an active response for the command.

Session # 10

BASE LINE			INTERVENTION		
M3	Jumping	1	M1	Give and take	3
			M2	Pick and drop	2
C2	Hello/Handshake	1	C1	Eye contact	4
G1	Scribbling	3			

The activities showed no variation from the previous session. All of them were given consistent scores.

Session # 11

BASE LINE			INTERVENTION		
M3	Jumping	1	M2	Pick and drop	3
C2	Hello / Handshake	1	C1	Eye contact	3
G1	Scribbling	3			

Sam had bowel complaint and was whining when brought to the school. The baseline assessment activities did not show any variation from the previous session.

Jumping: Did not evoke a response; hence scored 1.

Hello / Handshake: He looked away when greeted, with a blank expression. A score of 1 was given.

Scribbling: Sam scribbled with hand on hand support. A score of 3 was given.

Pick and drop: Sam now started making a better grip on the beads though he needed the leading physically and was reluctant to let go off the bead in the drop bowl. He was given a score of 3.

Eye contact: He started gritting his teeth and hitting his head when I asked him to look at me. So no more attempts were made. However, Sam made an evasive look when he had extreme irritability. He was scored 3.

Session # 12

	BASE LINE			INTERVENTION	
M3	Jumping	1	M2	Pick and drop	4
C2	Hello / Handshake	1	C1	Eye contact	5
G1	Scribbling	3			

The parent reported that the present day Sam was so relieved as he emptied his bowel. The baseline assessment activities did not show any variation from the previous session.

Pick and drop: Sam picked the beads one by one and dropped, without me leading him to do. A score of 4 was given. The boy seemed more attentive.

Eye contact: When he was cheered for performing the Pick and drop, he looked at me instantly and giggled back. He was given a score of 5 for the spontaneous response.

Session # 13

	BASE LINE			INTERVENTION	
M4	Texture sensing	1	M2	Pick and drop	4
			M3	Jumping	2
C3	oral-motor movement	1	C1	Eye contact	4
			C2	Hello / Handshake	2
G2	rolls play dough	2	G1	Scribbling	3

Hello / handshake: The usual Hello was accompanied by an extended hand. He was held at the door and he pushed me to let him. Unlike the previous days when I took his hands in mine, 'my' hand was held up to him. While the demand was persistent, I could see him looking at my hand. Sam made fists, drew back his hands and began pushing with head. When the demand seemed disturbing him I patted his shoulder and said 'you may come in, Sam'. Instantly, he grabbed my hands and pulled me into the room .He was given a score of 2 for the passive response with physical prompt.

Texture sensing: A sponge ball was given to Sam and he was asked to squeeze it (Figure 13). Sam sensed it with the tip of his finger and turned away. He did not show any further interest in the task even after repeated requests. He was given a score of 1.

Figure 13 Assistive Technique - Squeezing

Oral motor movements: Oral motor therapy works on the oral skills necessary for proper speech and feeding development. Tongue extension and later retraction were activities suggested by the Occupational therapist. For tongue extension Do like this – the action was modeled saying la la la tongue touching upper lip. In order to produce the /l/ sound, the tongue tip must elevate - to be exact – to the alveolar ridge (just behind the upper front teeth). It must also be able to function independently – or dissociate – from the jaw. Oral motor therapy works on these "pre-requisites" for speech and feeding. Sam did not bother to respond. Therefore was given a score of 1.

Rolls play dough: Children need and love play dough and messy play. It was introduced to reduce tactile sensitivity in Sam. The Occupational therapist reported that he avoided palm contact with people or objects. When presented the colored bottle of dough he peered at it but did not make any attempts at manipulating. Sam was asked to roll out the dough. After consistent prompting, he touched the dough very softly. The passive attempt made with physical prompting was given a score of 2.

Pick and drop: Sam now picks the beads one by one and drops in the bowl, without any prompting. A score of 4 was given.

Jumping: A trampoline was pulled down to the room and I started jumping on it. A rhyme "jump, jump, jump, and jump up high..." was sung along with the rhythm of the jumps. Sam giggled and came up to the device. I helped him climb. Sam seemed shivering and he clutched me tightly - Gravitational insecurity is defined as an emotional or fear reaction that is out of proportion to the vestibular proprioceptive stimuli or the position of the body in space. Aversive responses are hypothesized to be due to poor modulation of semicircular canal inputs (Fisher, Murray & Bundy, 1989).

When I said, "come on Sam, jump with me" he seemed to be scared. Therefore, I stood on the trampoline and made him sense the swing (up – down swing) of the device. For the passive response made with physical prompting for 'Jumping' a score of '2' was given. By and by, the grip on my hand loosened and he was more at ease.

Eye contact: In order to get an eye contact Sam needed multiple prompts. In between the trampoline jumping and pick and drop tasks he looked at me when I made a hum. Depending on the intonation and the presence or absence of glottal stops to shape the sound, a hum may signal agreement, disagreement, or simply acknowledgement. Sam was so keen on my humming and would make an instant checking when the humming was made. He was given a score of 4.

Scribbling: In order to improve his pattern of scribbling, music was played. The rhyme 'old Mc Donald's' was played and the therapist started making strokes on a large sheet of paper. The hand movements were in rhythm of the rhyme played. An up down motion was made with the crayons and Sam was asked to take the crayon and draw. When he did not pick up, hand on hand - assistance was again given. Sam drew with me in the usual way with the rhyme played in the background. He was scored 3 for the active response with physical prompting.

Session # 14

BASE LINE		INTERVENTION		
M4 Texture sensing	1	M2	Pick and drop	2
		M3	Jumping	2
C3 oral-motor movement	1	C1	Eye contact	4
		C2	Hello / Handshake	2
G2 rolls play dough	2	G1	Scribbling	3

Hello/handshake: Sam was held at the door with the extended hand demanding a handshake. His right palm was clasped before he made a fist and held it back as the other day. He grasped mine too in a reflex. The passive attempt made with physical prompting was scored 2.

Texture sensing: Sam took the ball lightly in his palms and dropped it back. He was scored 1.

Oral motor movements: He looked away even with repeated prompts. Therefore, he was scored 1.

Rolls play dough: Sam seemed attracted by the color or odor of the dough. However, he did not try to squeeze it. He touched mildly and pulled it back when prompted. A score of 2 was given.

Pick and drop: Sam was so reluctant to pick and drop the beads. It seemed as if he was getting bored of performing the task. He had to be prompted hand on hand to do the activity. The score was two.

Jumping: Sam was scared to climb on the trampoline. His balancing problem contributed to the anxiety he felt when asked to climb on. However, he wanted to be with me when I swung.. Sam clutched me tightly and enjoyed the up down motion, which was slowly led to jumps along with the rhyme. The passive responses with physical prompt were given 2 points.

Eye contact: Sam now looked whenever a verbal prompt was made. The active response with verbal prompt was scored 4.

Scribbling: The up down motion was made with the crayons and Sam was asked to take the crayon and draw with me. He did not pick up and hand on hand - assistance was given. The rhyme was played in the background. He was scored 3 for the active response with physical prompting.

Session # 15

BASE LINE		INTERVENTION	
M4 Texture sensing	2	M3 Jumping	2
C3 oral-motor movement	1	C2 Hello / Handshake	2
G2 rolls play dough	2	G1 Scribbling	3

Hello/handshake: Sam's right palm was clasped before he made a fist and held it back. He had no intention to initiate or make active response. The passive attempt made with physical prompting was scored 2 points.

Texture sensing: Sam took the ball lightly in his palms. With hand on hand assistance, he was prompted to press the ball. He molded the grasp on the ball but did not press. He was scored 2.

Oral motor movements: Sam closed his lips tightly when the task was introduced and he maintained the response intact throughout the session. He was scored one.

Rolls play dough: Sam did not try to squeeze or roll the dough. He touched it mildly and pulled back his palms making a fist when prompted. A score of 2 was given.

Jumping: His legs were shaky every time he climbed on the trampoline and attempted jumping, but he never resisted. The jumping was passive and needed much prompting physically. He was scored 2.

Scribbling: The rhyme was played in the background. He seemed interested in the rhythm played while the strokes were made. Eye contact seemed more sustaining on the paper and grip also was more firm but he stopped the scribble the moment the aid was receded. He was scored three for the active response with physical prompting.

Session # 16

BASE LINE		INTERVENTION	
M4 Texture sensing	1	M3 Jumping	2
C3 oral-motor movement	1	C2 Hello / Handshake	2
G2 rolls play dough	2	G1 Scribbling	4

Texture sensing: Sam was prompted to press the ball with hand on hand assistance, but he did not press. He curled his palms as if rejecting. Therefore, he was given the score 1.

Oral motor movements: Sam looked away every time a prompt was made to say 'la la la'. He was scored 1.

Rolls play dough: Sam touched the dough lightly when prompted. A score of 2 was given.

Jumping: The jumping was passive and much physical prompt was necessary. He was scored 2.

Hello / handshake: Passive attempts were made with physical prompting. He was scored 2.

Scribbling: The music was played and I started scribbling along with the music. He was peering amusingly at the rhythmic up, down movements I made. On later trials, he drew with verbal prompts. Although the strokes were vague, a score of 4 was given for the active attempts with verbal prompts.

Session # 17

BASE LINE		INTERVENTION	
M5 Sipping	1	M3 Jumping	2
		M4 Texture sensing	3
C4 Identify body part	1	C2 Hello / Handshake	2
		C3 oral-motor movement	2
G3 objectIdentification – receptive label	1	G1 Scribbling	4
		G2 rolls play dough	4

Hello/handshake: Greeting always was passive and needed physical prompting to obtain the slight response in the form of a molded palm in mine. A score of 2 was given.

Sipping: Sam stiffened his lips when a drink was taken close to his mouth. With the slightest smear of the food on lips, he would wipe up several times and hold the lip tightly shut. Sam was asked to sip water - like this and the activity was modeled. He turned away his face. A score of 1 was given.

Identify body part: Sam was asked Show me your foot. He made no response even after repeated trials and was given a score of 1.

Object Identification – receptive label: Models of two objects (a banana and a flower) were presented before Sam and he was asked to pick up. Sam picked the banana. But he made no response. The scoring did not vary for the flower also. He was given a score of 1.

Jumping: He needed physical prompt throughout; therefore, was scored 2.

Texture sensing: As the boy resisted pressing the sponge ball, additional stimulation was given. The ball was drenched in cold water and the therapist squeezed it out. Afterwards Sam was given another ball drenched in cold water. The temperature of the water was something recommended by the occupational therapist. However, Sam squeezed the ball to see the water dripping out of the ball. He was given a score of 3.

Oral motor movements: Honey was smeared on Sam's upper lip margin, his hands were gently held so that he would not wipe it off. He stooped down and wiped it on my dress. Next time he was held back and asked to lick it up, as modelled. He had the tickling on his lips and out of irritation, licked it up as modelled Sam seemed to dislike the intervention but the irritability shown subsided when he was held close and comforted. The passive response was scored 2.

Roll play dough: Sam had a dislike towards the sticky feeling of the dough. The parents complained that he would not take food (especially rice and dal – which is the only food he takes without complaint) with his hands. He would pull the parent's hand towards the plate if he were that hungry.

For the intervention, the dough was made sticky and his hands were pushed against it with my hand (Figure 14).

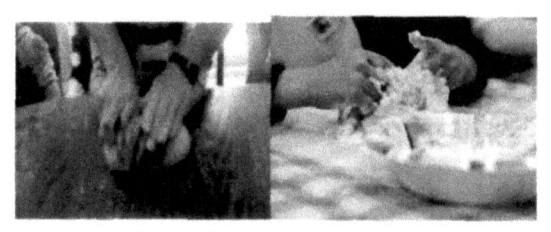

Figure 14 Assistive techniques - Kneading dough

He pushed me back when the hands became messy and started observing the dough on his palms and how it stuck when he curled his palms. Gradually he got accustomed to the sensation and started rolling the dough. By the end of the session, Sam rolled the dough along with my verbal prompt. He was given a score of 4.

Scribbling: when the music was played, he drew with verbal prompts. Although the strokes were vague, a score of 4 was given for the active attempts with verbal prompts.

Session # 18

BASE LINE		INTERVENTION	
M5 Sipping	1	M3 Jumping	2
		M4 Texture sensing	3
C4 Identify body part	1	C2 Hello / Handshake	2
		C3 oral-motor movement	2
G3 Object Identification -- receptive	1	G1 Scribbling	4
		G2 rolls play dough	4

Baseline activities as well as the intervened activities yielded consistent scores as the previous session.

Session # 19

BASE LINE		INTERVENTION	
M5 Sipping	1	M4 Texture sensing	4
C4 Identify body part	1	C3 oral-motor movement	2
G3 Object Identification	1	G2 rolls play dough	3

Sipping, Identify body part, and Object identification did not elicit any response from the kid.

Texture sensing: Sam now squeezed out water from the ball when asked to do so. A score of 4 was given.

Oral motor movements: Tongue protrusion was done out of necessity and after much prompting. A score of 2 was given.

Roll play dough: Sam needed physical prompting to do the rolling and was scored 3 for the co – operation he showed.

Session # 20

BASE LINE		INTERVENTION	
M5 Sipping	1	M4 Texture sensing	4
C4 Identify body part	1	C3 oral-motor movement	3
G3 Object Identification – receptive	1	G2 rolls play dough	4

Sipping: He disliked any intervention in or around his mouth and always shook off his head. He was scored 1.

Identify body part: When asked 'show your foot' he sat blank faced with no response. A score of 1 was given.

Object identification: He would not pick up or touch the object when asked to do so. A score of 1 was given again.

Texture sensing: Sam now felt the sponge ball in his hands and squeezed to see whether water was left in it or not. The active attempt with verbal prompt was given a score of 4.

Oral motor movements: Sam's irritability towards the honey smearing reduced when he was held close. He protruded his tongue with the physical prompt. A score of 3 was given.

Roll play dough: Sam rolls the dough with pressure and was found manipulating it with the fingers also, but needed verbal prompts to try it out. A score of 4 was given.

Session # 21

BASE LINE		INTERVENTION	
		M4 Texture sensing	5
		M5 Sipping	2
C5 high five	2	C3 oral-motor movement	3
		C4 Identify body part	3
G4 peg board	1	G2 rolls play dough	3
		G3 Object Identification – receptive	2

High five: (Figure 15). The task was taken from the Curriculum Guide (Maurice, 1996). Sam was now showing some readiness in sensing with his palms. Hence, a task that would help to show a celebratory gesture was introduced. He seemed unfamiliar and disinterested as usual. He looked at me when the usual jubilation for his success in a task (sponge ball squeezing) was followed by a raised hand and I said "Give me five". When he was prompted physically to slap on my hand he looked away and grimaced. On later trials, his hand was more yielding. The passive response was scored 2.

Figure 15 Assistive technique - high five

Pegboard: To improve fine motor skills and enhance attention and eye contact, the task was introduced. Sam used to pick up things but the grip was loose. The pegboard was kept on the table and he was asked to insert the pegs into it. He was shown how to do and was asked, "Sam let us put these pegs into the hole, like this?" He walked away deftly avoiding my attempts to hold his hands. He was given a score of 1.'

Texture sensing: Sam was hyper reactive to the feeling of the sponge ball which he now picked up and manipulated well with his palms. He did not wait for the prompts even. Hence a score of 5 was given.

Sipping: The glass of water was held outside his teeth margin and tilted to his mouth. He was asked close lips and drink. Sam rejected the task with all his strength. Later the boy was comforted and seated close to me so that his hands were held down gently with one hand and the water was offered with the other. The space also limited him from escaping. The therapist modeled sipping with a transparent glass of water. Sam breathed through his mouth as he was straining to avoid the oral stimulation. He made stiffened retracted lips and drew in some water. Warm applause was given and Sam gave a sweeping glance at me. The passive attempt with physical prompting is scored 2.

Oral motor movements: Sam protruded his tongue with physical prompt. A score of 3 was given.

Identify body part: Sam was asked to show his foot. In order to intervene his response repertoire his shoes were brought in and therapist sat down as if to put it on. Then he was asked, 'show me your foot' and he extended his foot to me. It was well appreciated and the task was repeated saying 'Where is Sam's foot?' He does not respond. It was noticed that Sam made active attempts with physical prompt. He was scored three.

Roll play dough: The dough rolling needed verbal prompt and it was a passive attempt. A score of three was given.

Objects Identification – receptive label: Sam did not seem to be associating the label to the object. He was shown the gesture of smelling a flower, and shown the flower. A chewing gesture was made and shown the banana. Sam was watching when the exaggerated facial expressions were made for chewing and smelling. Afterwards he was asked Sam, Give flower. He was still passive but responded with much physical prompting. No variation in performance was noticed for the Banana also. A score of two was given.

Session # 22

BASE LINE		INTERVENTION	
		M4 Texture sensing	5
		M5 Sipping	3
C5 high five	2	C3 oral-motor movement	4
		C4 Identify body part	3
G4 peg board	2	G2 rolls play dough	4
		G3 object Identification	4

High five: Sam needed physical prompt to slap on my hand but his expression showed curiosity. The gesture was not familiar; hence, it had to be introduced along with the jubilation made contiguous to the successful approximation in some task and worked on. On later trials, his hand was more yielding. The passive response was scored 2.

Pegboard: Sam noticed me doing the peg insertion saying 'press it down'. He took a peg and placed it on the board. The trials required intense prompting and he was given a score of 2.

Texture sensing: Sam picked up the sponge ball and squeezed it the moment it was given. A score of 5 was given.

Sipping: Even before the drink was presented, an attempt was made to encourage the child through comments about the way he responded the previous day. At times, it worked with the boy. The reinforcement given made him more yielding. The physical prompting and restraining were there but he made a better effort. The drawing in of the liquid was scored 3.

Oral motor movements: Honey was smeared on his lip. He immediately licked up. A score of 4 was given.

Identify body part: He was asked "Sam's foot?" No response was obtained. The prompting continued and on later trials, he jerked his foot when the verbal prompt was given. A score of 3 was given.

Roll play dough: Sam rolled out the dough on command. A score of 4 was given.

Objects Identification – receptive label: Sam easily responded to the verbal prompts. He picked and gave the flower as well as the fruit. He was given a score of 4 points.

Session # 23

BASE LINE		INTERVENTION	
C5 high five	2	M5 Sipping	4
		C4 Identify body part	4
G4 peg board	1	G3 object Identification – receptive label	4

High five: Sam needed physical prompt to slap on my hand. The passive response was scored two.

Pegboard: Sam did not want to do the task. He kept on pushing away the board. The blank response was given a score of 1.

Sipping: Sam got accustomed to the sipping task and seemed less rebellious. He was making retraction of lip as well as tongue but his head was leaning forward earnestly. It was well reinforced and on later trials, he sipped on command. The score was 4

Identify body part: Sam jerked his foot, when asked. The score was 4.

Object identification: He picks up the flower and fruit on command. A score of 4 was given.

Session # 24

BASE LINE			INTERVENTION	
			M5 Sipping	4
C5 high five		2	C4 Identify body part	4
G4 peg board		1	G3 object Identification – receptive label	4

All the tasks yielded consistent scores as the previous session.

Session # 25

BASE LINE			INTERVENTION	
			M5 Sipping	4
			C4 Identify body part	4
			C5 high five	3
G5 coloring		1	G3 object Identification – receptive label	4
			G4 peg board	2

Coloring: Filling a shape with color was the task chosen. Sam was given a circle and asked to color it. As he used to do the scribbling on command, it was expected that he would start instantly, but the long gap in between the sessions (almost one month) must have made him disinterested. He did not pick up the crayon even after the prompts. A score of 1 was given.

Sipping: He sipped on command, hence scored 4.

Identify body part: Sam moved foot when asked "Sam's foot?" A score of 4 was given.

High five: Sam expected the physical prompt for slap and found my raised hand and a verbal prompt of "Come on Sam", instead. As it was planned to up heave his response pattern in the High five task it was introduced only for the seemingly most pleasant or active moments of the boy. When he moved his foot for the previous task the high five was given. He made a spontaneous jerk of hand, as if to meet mine and curled his fists to inhibit a response. A firm hug was given as a sign of reassurance. On later trials, though a physical lead was given, Sam raised his palms up to mine. He was scored 3.

Object identification: He picked up the objects on command. A score of 4 was given.

Pegboard: "Put these pegs into the mat and go" was said and I started writing to show that I am no more concerned. I could see him watching me intently, and after some time started manipulating the pegs. He started dropping pegs deliberately on the floor looking at me. I picked up the pegs, inserted five of them in a row, and gave him the bowl with a nod of head to continue. He picked a peg reluctantly (it takes a lot of time and immense patience to remain unaffected. The slightest provocation would end up in whimpering and rejection of the task). A score of two was given for the passive response. Immediately after that he was let go.

Session # 26

BASE LINE		INTERVENTION	
		M5 Sipping	4
		C4 Identify body part	4
		C5 high five	4
G5 coloring	1	G3 object Identification – receptive label	3
		G4 peg board	3

Coloring a shape: As the baseline of coloring was being measured, no attempts at helping him recollect the previous task (Scribbling) was given. Sam seemed disinterested. When physically prompted he picks up the crayon and scribbles. However, the scribbling is made irrespective of the picture drawn. A score of 1 was given

Sipping: He sipped on command, hence scored 4.

Identify body part: Sam showed his foot when asked. A score of 4 was given.

High five: Sam raised his hand to the level of mine if repeatedly given a verbal prompting. A score of 4 was given.

Object identification: Sam was reluctant to do the tasks. He demanded physical prompting. A score of 3 was given.

Pegboard: When the "put these pegs into the mat and go," comment was made, a surge in interest was noticed. Somehow, he wants to do the task and escape from the room. This time he made active attempts with physical prompting. Help was needed to hold the peg up right. A score of 3 was given.

Session # 27

BASE LINE		INTERVENTION	
		C5 high five	5
G5 coloring	1	G4 peg board	4

Coloring: Sam did not do the coloring inside the shape. A score of 1 was given.

High five: Sam raised his hand spontaneously when he was cheered for putting the pegs in the mat. A score of 5 was given.

Pegboard: Sam puts a few pegs (two to three) with much effort. He requires affirmation as humming from me. A score of 4 was given with much appreciation.

Session # 28

BASE LINE		INTERVENTION	
G5 coloring	1	C5 high five	4
		G4 peg board	4

Coloring: Sam did not do the coloring inside the shape. A score of one was given.

Pegboard: The task was done with verbal prompt. A score of 4 was given.

High five: Sam raised hand when said, "hey high five!" A score of 4 was given.

Session # 29

BASE LINE	INTERVENTION	
	C5 high five	4
	G4 peg board	4
	G5 coloring	2

Sam did the pegboard task and the high five with verbal prompt. A score of 4 was given.

Coloring: For intervention in the task, the rhyme was played again and the modeling was done as circular strokes along the border of the circle and later filling up the pattern. Sam sat watching. On further attempts, he did the task with physical prompting. The passive response with prompting was given a score of 2.

Session # 30

BASE LINE	INTERVENTION	
	C5 high five	4
	G4 peg board	5
	G5 coloring	2

Pegboard task was done spontaneously and a score of 5 was given. High five was performed when verbally prompted and a score of 4 was given. Coloring needed physical prompting as he found it difficult to control his strokes within the limits of the shape. A score of 2 was given.

Session # 31

BASE LINE	INTERVENTION	
	G5 coloring	3

Coloring: As per the demand of the research design, no other tasks were given in the session. This left plenty of trials temporally together for attempting the coloring. The boy does actively but reaches out to my hand for support. A score of 3 was given.

Session # 32

BASE LINE	INTERVENTION	
	G5 coloring	3

Coloring: No escalation in performance noticed from the previous session. A score of 3 was given.

Session # 33

BASE LINE	INTERVENTION	
	G5 coloring	4

Coloring: Sam did the circular strokes a bit more carefully without the physical support. This was well reinforced. A score of 4 was given.

Session # 34

BASE LINE	INTERVENTION	
	G5 coloring	4

Coloring: He needed verbal prompting to control rhythm of his motor response. A score of 4 was given.

The scores for response strength of Second Participant – Sam over the three month period is condensed and listed in Table 5 .

3.4.4. Reliability of the procedure

All research carries the responsibility of convincing oneself and one's audience that the findings are based on critical investigation. Reliability concerns the replication of the study under similar circumstances. It pertains to issues such as training interviewers and systematically recording and transcribing data.

Inter observer agreement is the most commonly used indicator of measurement quality in applied behavior analysis. Inter observer agreement refers to the degree to which two or more independent observers report the same observed values after measuring the same events (Cooper et al., 2014). A valid assessment of Inter observer agreement depends on three criteria:

- Observers must use the same measurement system
- Observers must measure the same participants, and
- Observers must be independent.

Here the Observer was scheduled to do an assessment session of the children after the Researcher's session series – on baseline as well as intervention phase. A single score was given to Baseline as well as Intervention Phases of each activity by the observer.

The Observer's score was then compared against the median score provided by the experimenter for the baseline and intervention sessions.

3.5. Statistical Approaches

3.5.1. Inter Observer Agreement

The scores provided for the two participants by the researcher and observer are tabulated and compared. The baseline scores and intervention scores of the two for the activities were compared using the Wilcoxon signed-rank test.

The Wilcoxon Signed Rank procedure is used to compare two sets of scores that come from the same participants. This can occur when we wish to investigate any change in scores from one time point to another, or when individuals are subjected to more than one condition. The test assumes that the sample we have is randomly taken from a population, with a symmetric frequency distribution. The symmetric assumption does not assume normality, simply that there seems to be roughly the same number of values above and below the median. The Wilcoxon procedure computes a test statistic W_{STAT} that is compared to an expected value. W_{STAT} is computed by summing the ranked differences of the deviation of each variable from a hypothesized median above the hypothesized value.

Table 5 The scores for response strength of second participant

Activity/SessionNo	1	2	3	4	5	6	7	8	9	10	11	12	13	14	15	16	17	18	19	20	21	22	23	24	25	26	27	28	29	30	31	32	33	34
M1 Give & take	2	2	1	2	3	3	5	3	3	3																								
C1 Eye contact	1	1	2	2	2	2	2	2	4	4	3	5	4	4																				
G1 Scribbling	2	3	2	3	3	3	3	3	3	3	3	3	3	3	3	4	4	4																
M2 Pick & drop					1	1	1	1	2	2	3	4	4	2																				
C2 Hello/Handshke										1	1	1	2	2	2	2	2	2				4												
G2 Rolling dough													2	2	2	2	4	4	3	4	3													
M3 Jumping									1	1		1	2	2	2	2	2	2																
C3 Oral-motormovt.													1	1	1	1	2	2	2	3	3	4												
G3 Object Idntfction																		1	1	1	2	4	4	4	4	3								
M4 Texture sensing													1	1	2	1	3	3	4	4	5	5	4	4	4	4								
C4 Body part																	1	1	1	1	3	3	4	1	2	4	4	4	4	5				
G4 Peg board																					1	2	1	1	2	3	4	1	2	2	1			
M5 Sipping																		1			2	3	4	4	4	4	5	4	4	4				
C5 High five																					2	2	2	2	3	4	1	1	2	2	3	3	4	4
G5 Coloring																									1	1	1							4

Baseline / Intervention

3.5.2. Visual Analysis

The phases of a Single-subject design are usually summarized on a graph. The data facilitates monitoring and evaluating the impact of the intervention. When interpreting graphically displayed behavioral data, **visual analysis** is used (Cooper et al, 2007). Visual analysis is a "systematic approach for interpreting the results of behavioral research and treatment programs that entails visual inspection of graphed data for variability, level, and trend within and between experimental conditions."

When the data is plotted, there are three properties that are used to identify what is "going on" with the data; these are the variability, the level, and the trend.

Variability: The variability of data relates to how different or "spread out" the scores are from each other.

Level: The level of the data relates to the "position" of the data set taken from the Y-axis. Mean level lines are horizontal lines drawn through the series of data points for the different research phases. They are used to see the summary of average performance within a phase (Cooper et al, 2007, p. 151). In this study, since the scores are ordinal data, **Median level lines** were used and compared to each other. The median level of a set of points is a line that has half the points above and half the points below.

Trend: The trend in the data is the "direction" it is going. They describe the overall direction that is taken by a data path (Cooper et al, 2007). According to Cooper, in a given data set, trend lines can be drawn using a linear regression formula, which describes the overall trend of the data. A trend occurs when the scores may be either increasing or decreasing during the baseline period. The direction of the line indicates whether the target behavior is decreasing or increasing. The slope of the line indicates the rate in which the behavior is increasing or decreasing. Several procedures have been described for calculating estimates of trends in data. All trend estimation procedures are used to make judgments about changes in level and trend, but they do not produce statements of statistical significance. Examples of such procedures include the semi average method, the least squares method, the median slope procedure, and the split-middle procedure.

The split-middle method of trend estimation is calculated easily without a computer and its predictive validity is known (Wolery & Harris,1982). Hence, the Split – middle line trend is taken for the study. All data points are considered in trend line calculation even if the resulting display does not appear so.

White (1971; 1974) first proposed the 'split - middle trend line', otherwise known as the 'quickie split - middle technique.' It is a method for devising the trend (or slope) within each phase presented on a graph (as cited in CBER, 2010, Feb 17). The specific steps used to compute a trend line using the split-middle method have been presented extensively in the single-subject literature (Stocks, 2008) and are not repeated here. The basic steps involve splitting the data into two halves, calculating the means of each half and then plotting the data points to fit the trend line.

3.5.2.1 The Behavior Modification Program

While taking multiple baselines across behaviors in the present study, continuous measures of the proceeding tiers were taken without waiting for one tier of activity to finish, i.e. no temporal distinction was made between tiers of activities under study. In the particular design if the technical methods are to be rigidly followed, the subject would be presented with only two tiers (six activities) in the stipulated time, i.e., three months. This also means that the baseline assessment of third activity in a tier should proceed for 12 sessions without even prompting the child. Hence, the researcher introduced the activities one after the other in such a way that once the baseline assessment of the first motor activity was over baseline assessment of the second motor activity began along with the intervention of the former. This has led to the overlapping of tiers of activities better noticeable in the intervention plan given in table 2 and 4.

The compromise in research design was necessary when it was noticed that the child was becoming complacent. A distinction has to be made between being compliant and being complacent. Many individuals, especially ones who have spent considerable time completing discrete trial drills, merely go through the motions. They are not actively involved with their environments. They have simply been trained to make certain responses to certain cues. When a complacent individual begins to protest and whine when given directions, it indicates that he is trying to communicate. He is also developing awareness that his behavior can have an impact on his environment. The therapist should make the most of every opportunity for the child with special need if the child has to be successful in learning skills.

Considering the intensive time consuming and less productive nature of the design, this modification was introduced. In addition, ethical considerations make it unacceptable to delay treatment for the other children in the school. History effects and generalization of effects of the activities are obvious in several sessions and the only measure taken to control is avoiding contiguous presentation.

3.5.2.1.1 Line graphs:

Line diagrams are used to summarize the results. The variation in the magnitude of response is observed by analyzing the variability within and across baseline and intervention phase, change in median level and the trend of the performance. The line graphs are a remarkably versatile vehicle for displaying behavior change and hence are used to display the results of the intervention in the study. The black dotted lines indicate the phase change from Baseline to Intervention. Arrow headed dotted lines indicate variation in the median level. The green lines are indicative of the trend of the scores in either phase of the study.

3.5.2.1.2 Effect Size:

Non-overlap of All Pairs Method (NAP Method)

Effect size is a numerical way of expressing the strength or magnitude of a reported relationship, be it causal or not (Whalberg, 1984). In single subject research, many meta-analyses have been conducted to draw conclusions about the overall effectiveness of interventions. The amount of change with known precision is best accomplished by an effect size index. Two types of strategies have been proposed for assessing the magnitude of effect in single-subject research: regression and non-regression approaches. Non-regression models include simpler non-overlap methods (Parker, Vannest, & Davis, 2011).

All non-overlap methods share the benefit of blending well with visual analysis of graphed data. In addition, all non-overlap techniques are easy to use. They all can be calculated with a pencil from a data plot. Non-overlap of All Pairs Method (NAP) was developed mainly to improve upon existing single case research overlap-based methods: Percentage of Non-overlapping Data (PND), Percentage of all Non-overlapping Data (PAND), and Percentage of Data Exceeding the Median (PEM). Non overlap of all pairs (NAP) is interpreted as the percentage of all pair wise comparisons across baseline and treatment phase, which show improvement across phases or, more simply, the percentage of data, which improve across phases (Parker, Vannest, & Davis, 2011). A simpler wording is the percent of non-overlapping data between baseline and treatment phases. The concept of score overlap is identical to that used by visual analysts of single case research graphs and is the same as is calculated in the other overlap indices, PAND, PEM and PND (Parker & Vannest, 2009). NAP is a "complete" non-overlap index as it individually compares all baseline and treatment phase data points (Parker, Vannest, & Davis, 2011).

In order to find the NAP manually, the number of data points in phase A and phase B are multiplied together to obtain the total number of paired comparison. Next, the overlap zone is visually identified by finding the lowest phase B data point and the highest phase A data point. All data in the zone is an overlap and will be counted as negative. Data, which are identical in value, will be counted as a tie. The fastest way to calculate is to find the negatives and subtract from total number of pairs to get the number of positives (Pos). The Number of positives added to half (.5) the number of ties, and divided by the no of pairs gives the NAP value (Parker, Vannest, & Davis, 2011).

$$NAP = \frac{Pos + (.5 \times no.\ of\ Ties)}{No.\ of\ Pairs}$$

The NAP calculator, which is web based calculator for Single Case Research analysis is used to find out the effect size (Vannest, Parker & Gonen, 2011). Parker and Vannest (2009) offer a tentative NAP range based on visual judgments of 200 data sets: weak effects: 0–.65; medium effects: .66–.92; large or strong effects: .93–1.0. Transforming NAP to a zero chance level gives these corresponding ranges: weak effects: 0–.31; medium effects: .32–.84; large or strong effects: .85–1.0. The specific steps are elaborated in the single case research literature (ref. Parker & Vannest, 2009).

3.5.2.2. Pre-post test score comparison of the sensory index profile:

Assessment using the Sensory integration inventory was repeated to make comparisons between pre and post intervention performance. The Occupational therapist assessed the sensory integration of the children taking into account the information from the parents. Histograms of the profiles of the two children were then charted and visually analyzed for the variations present.

The bar graph or histograms are plotted to compare the Pre test Post test scores of the experimental as well as control group in the Sensory Index profile. Histogram is a simple and versatile format for graphically summarizing behavioral data. It gives a visual summary of the performance of a participant during the different conditions of an experiment.

Interpretation

In interpreting histograms, if the plotted data points fall into the top section of the plot area they would have a "high level", if they fell into the middle section, they would have a "moderate level" and if they were in the bottom section, they would have a "low level". The data levels can further be divided into "low-to-moderate" or "moderate-to-high" (Cooper, Heron, & Heward, 2007).

The assessment was done by the Occupational therapist after gathering essential details from the parents and special educator. The results are entered in Table 21. A score equal to zero suggests that the individual is free of sensory problems and a score above zero is indicative of its presence.

Comparison of the Difference Scores: A simple comparison of the changing variable scores was done by computing post minus pre scores and then the two groups are compared based on those difference scores. Difference score or Gain score is an intuitively appealing technique for predicting change. The method is to compute the difference in the outcome variable between time 1 and time 2 and then use the different score as the dependent variable (Robins, Fraley & Krueger, 2007). Such a method appears to measure change, because time-1 score on the outcome are subtracted from time-2 scores on the outcome so that positive numbers indicate increases in the outcome and negative numbers indicate decline in the outcome. Here the variable measured is sensitivity, where a score above zero is indicative of its presence. Therefore, a decline indicates improvement in the functioning of the child.

The results after analysis of the data and the discussions thereof are presented in the next chapter.

4. RESULTS AND DISCUSSION

4.1 Inter Observer Agreement

4.2 Visual analysis

Assessment of children with autism must be especially sensitive to the subtle qualities rather than obvious deficiencies observed in their behavior. Recognizing development as a transformational process rather than as a series of successive stages allows us to alter our perceptions of normalcy. In this way, we interpret all behavior, even unconventional perceptions in play as purposeful and adaptive, as meaningful attempts to initiate independent social activities. Observations of child initiations even in unusual forms may serve as indices of present and emerging abilities. Assessing in this way is essential for guiding our decisions as to how to intervene (Scottish Intercollegiate Guidelines Network, 2007).

An ordered environment is a great comfort to children with autism and adds to independent behavior. Even though these same principles apply to anyone, they are *essential* for the person with autism. Living in an environment that is disorganizing or where people make constant changes and do not respect the needs of the child is frustrating and impedes learning. The children subjected to intervention were given an ordered environment, respecting their needs and to facilitate learning.

Many different angles and aspects of the collected data are analyzed and compared, in answering the research questions. Firstly, the credibility of the scoring procedure was verified. Secondly, the efficacy of the intervention procedure was checked by visual analysis of line graphs and statistical analysis using Non overlapping Pairs Method for effect size estimation. Finally, a pre post temporal variation of the sensory profile of the four children who participated in the study was compared.

4.1. Inter-Observer Agreement

Just as scientific records can be vulnerable to variation between different pieces of recording equipment, so observational records are subject to differences in how observers score behavior. However, one can judge how much confidence to place in one's results by assessing the reliability of the records of one's variables. All agree that inter observer agreement is the bedrock upon which sound behavioral measurement rests (Cone, 1977 ; Suen, 1988). Numerous methods of assessing inter observer agreement have been developed, applied, and debated over the past two decades. Most prominent among these indices are percent agreement (including occurrence/nonoccurrence percent agreement) and kappa.

In the study, the two raters tacitly agreed about the 'improvement' of the children through multisensory stimulation. However, assessment of a score by score-agreement between the raters (researcher as well as the observer) alone would not yield a favorable result. Hence, the scores given by the two raters for the list of activities under two conditions- baseline and intervention were considered as repeated measures design and the Wilcoxon Signed Ranks Test was done. The median of scores given by the researcher is listed and compared with the score given by the observer and analyzed (see appendix for the data subjected for Wilcoxon Signed Ranks Test).

4.1.1. Participant 1 – Aman

A Wilcoxon matched pairs signed rank test was conducted to determine whether there was a difference in the rating given by the researcher and observer in the baseline as well as the post intervention phase of first participant – Aman for the 21 activities given.

Table 6 shows the descriptive statistics and inferences drawn from Wilcoxon Signed Ranks test of first participant's scores given by the researcher and observer in the baseline as well as post intervention phase.

Table 6 Inter observer agreement of first participant's scores

	Pairs	No of activities	Mean	Standard Dev.	Test statistic(z)	p value
Baseline	Researcher's score	21	2.3810	.83524	-1.517	.129
	Observer's score	21	2.1429	.91026		
Intervention	Researcher's score	21	3.9524	.56800	.680	.497
	Observer's score	21	3.8571	.72703		

Comparison of the baseline scores indicate that there was no significant difference (z= -1.517, p > .05) between the pairs of scores assigned by the researcher and the observer. Scores given by the researcher and observer for the various activities during the post intervention phase of the subject also indicates that there was no significant difference (z = -.680, p > .05) in how the researcher and observer scored the activities for Aman during the post intervention phase.

4.1.2. Participant 2 – Sam

Wilcoxon matched pairs signed rank test was conducted to determine whether there was a difference in the scoring of baseline as well as the post intervention phase of second participant – Sam in 15 activities by the researcher and observer.

Table 7 shows the descriptive statistics and inferences from Wilcoxon Signed Ranks test of the second participant's scores given by the researcher and observer in the baseline as well as post intervention phase.

Table 7 Inter observer agreement of second participant's scores

	Pairs	No of activities	Mean	Standard Dev.	Test statistic(z)	p value
Baseline	Researcher's score	15	1.4000	.63246	.000	1.000
	Observer's score	15	1.4000	.63246		
Intervention	Researcher's score	15	3.3667	.78982	-1.566	.120
	Observer's score	15	2.9333	.70373		

Results indicated that there was no difference (z = .000, p > .05) between the scores assigned by the researcher and the observer for the second participant in the baseline function of behavior modification program focusing on multisensory stimulation procedure.

Comparison of the intervention scores also indicate that there was no significant difference (z = -1.566, p > .05) in how the researcher and observer scored the activities in the post intervention phase.

The following inferences were drawn from the analyses:

1. There is no significant difference between the scores assigned by the researcher and the observer for the performance of the first participant in the behavior modification program focusing on multisensory stimulation procedure.

2. There is no significant difference between the scores assigned by the researcher and the observer for the performance of the second participant in the behavior modification program focusing on multisensory stimulation procedure.

4.2. Visual analysis

This section details the analysis of the behavior modification program as well as the variation in the pre post levels of the sensory profile of the four children.

4.2.1 The Behavior Modification Program

Interpretation of line graphs showing the nature of the levels and trends shown by the first and second participants in the motor, communicative and cognitive domains across the baseline and intervention phases is detailed in the following pages. The line graphs show the score distribution, the median level of performance, change in trend of scores and overlap zone (if present). The score base for plotting the graphs are entered in the corresponding tables.

4.2.1.1 Participant 1 – Aman

The response pattern of the first participant in the motor, communicative and cognitive domains across the baseline and intervention phases is detailed below.

4.2.1.1.1 First tier of activities: M1C1G1

Figure 16 illustrates the line graph showing first participant's response in the first tier.

Table 8 details the distribution of scores for the first tier of activities.

M1 -Jumping. Aman scored 'one' consistently over the four baseline sessions. This shows a stable trend in performance as shown in the graphs. After the phase change, the scores show an upward trend. The level of performance has gone up two points (a shift from one to three). The final score showed that the boy has made active response with verbal prompt that initially had been 'no response' even with physical prompting. There is a within phase variation of scores in the Intervention, ranging from two to four showing marked improvement in response.

C1- Hello / Handshake Aman used to make passive attempts with physical prompting in order to make a greeting. He scored 'two' consistently over the baseline phase, making a stable trend in performance as shown in the graphs. After the phase change also the score has shown a stable trend but at an elevated level. The level of performance has improved by two points (a shift from two to four). The response pattern became an active response with a verbal prompt.

G1- Scribbling: It was a consistent level of passive response across the baseline. It needs to be noticed that after the 10th session a hike in the baseline level has occurred. The graphs in Figure16 show that when the second tier of activity (Hello/ Hand shake) was introduced a simultaneous shift in the data pattern occurred for the target behavior in the third tier (Scribbling). While it could be interpreted as an extraneous event in the environment (history effect) that happened to coincide with the end of the second baseline, an alternate rival explanation is also possible.

When multiple baselines are applied across behaviors, a data pattern like this could also be due to generalization of effects (Rubin & Babbie, 2011). Generalization of effects occurs when an intervention, although intended to apply to only one behavior at a time, affects other target behaviors that are still in the baseline phase as soon as it is applied to the first behavior. Another way that generalization of effects could occur is when the intervention affects only one target behavior but the change in that behavior changes the other behaviors in turn. In the current situation, it should be recalled that Aman was very much eager to do the trampoline jumping

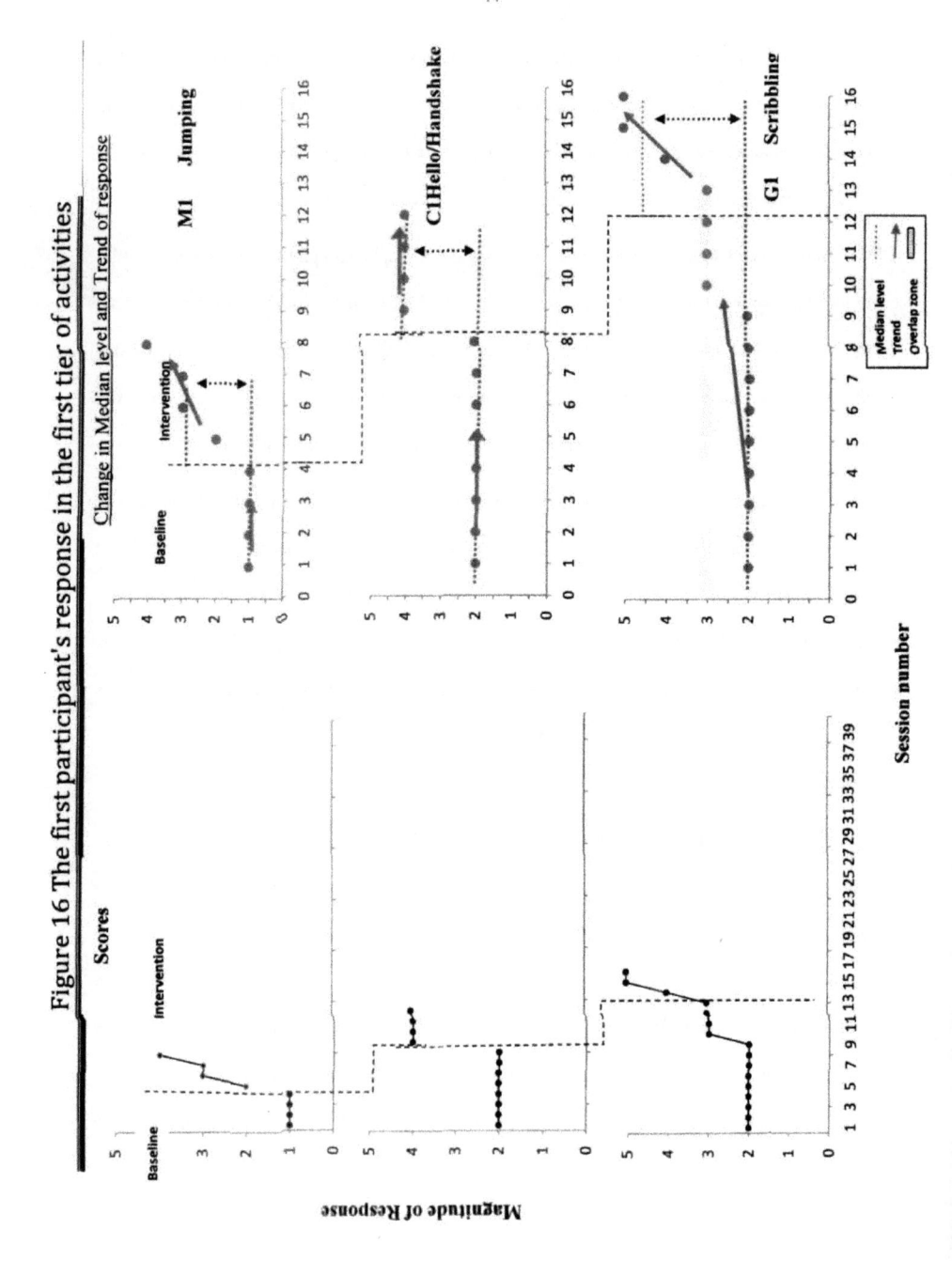

Figure 16 The first participant's response in the first tier of activities

and the less preferred activities in the same tier (Hello/ Hand shake and Scribbling) were performed in a haste to get back to the preferred activity. Moreover, the rewarding nature of the feedback he received even for his fumbling attempts could have also increased his desire to act appropriately.

When the task was intervened, scores showed a gradual upward trend. The median level shows a hike of 2.5 score points across the phases. The task was performed by Aman independently after the 16th session. A within phase variation of two points (3 to 5) is seen revealing the progressive response pattern.

Table 8 The distribution of scores of the first participant for the first tier of activities.

Session no.		1	2	3	4	5	6	7	8	9	10	11	12	13	14	15	16
M1	Score	1	1	1	1	2	3	3	4								
	Trend	1	to	1		2.5	to	3.5									
	Median (Level)		1				3										
	NAP					1				90% CI* = .288 < > 1.7							
C1	Score	2	2	2	2	2	2	2	2	4	4	4	4				
	Trend		2		to		2			4	to	4					
	Median (Level)				2						4						
	NAP					1				90% CI = .395 < > 1.605							
G1	Score	2	2	2	2	2	2	2	2	2	3	3	3	3	4	5	5
	Trend		2		to		2							3.5	to	5	
	Median (Level)				2										4.5		
	NAP				.97					90% CI = .372 < > 1.503							

* Confidence Interval

Effect Size

Here M1 and C1 had a stable base line and no values in the intervention phase of the design shows an overlapping. The extent to which data in the baseline versus intervention phases do not overlap is an accepted indicator of the amount of performance change. Therefore, there is absolute improvement in scores. We can be 90% certain that the true effect size lies somewhere between .28 and 1.7 for M1 and between .395 and 1.605 for C1. In G1 there is overlapping of scores. NAP is calculated as .97, which is a strong effective change and the true effect size lies between .372 and 1.5.

4.2.1.1.2 Second tier of activities: M2C2G2

Figure 17 illustrates the line graph showing first participant's response in the second tier.

Table 9 details the distribution of scores of the first participant for the second tier of activities.

M2-Blowing: The baseline performance of the boy varied one point showing an upward trend. The hike in the baseline should also be suspected due to the generalisation effect of the intervention given for the M1 (Trampoline jumps) in the sixth session. The child was so excited that it gave a fillip to his performance with the other tasks. The median level of performance was two, which was shifted to three point five in the intervention phase. The trend was steeply up with the intervention. The child blew spontaneously in the 12th session without prompting.

Table 9. The distribution of scores of the first participant for the second tier of activities.

Session no.		5	6	7	8	9	10	11	12	13	14	15	16	17	18	19	20
M2	Score	1	2	2	2	3	3	4	5								
	Trend		1.5 to 2			3 to 4.5											
	Median (Level)		2			3.5											
	NAP				1					90% CI = .288<>1.7							
C2	Score					2	3	3	3	4	5	5	5				
	Trend					2.5 to 3				4.5 to 5							
	Median (Level)					3				5							
	NAP				1					90% CI = .288<>1.7							
G2	Score									3	3	4	4	4	4	4	5
	Trend									3 to 4				4 to 4.5			
	Median (Level)									3.5				4			
	NAP					.81				90% CI = -.087<>1.337							

C2 - Give and Take: The baseline was showing a median level score of three indicating Aman making active attempts with physical prompting. The intervention lifted the level of

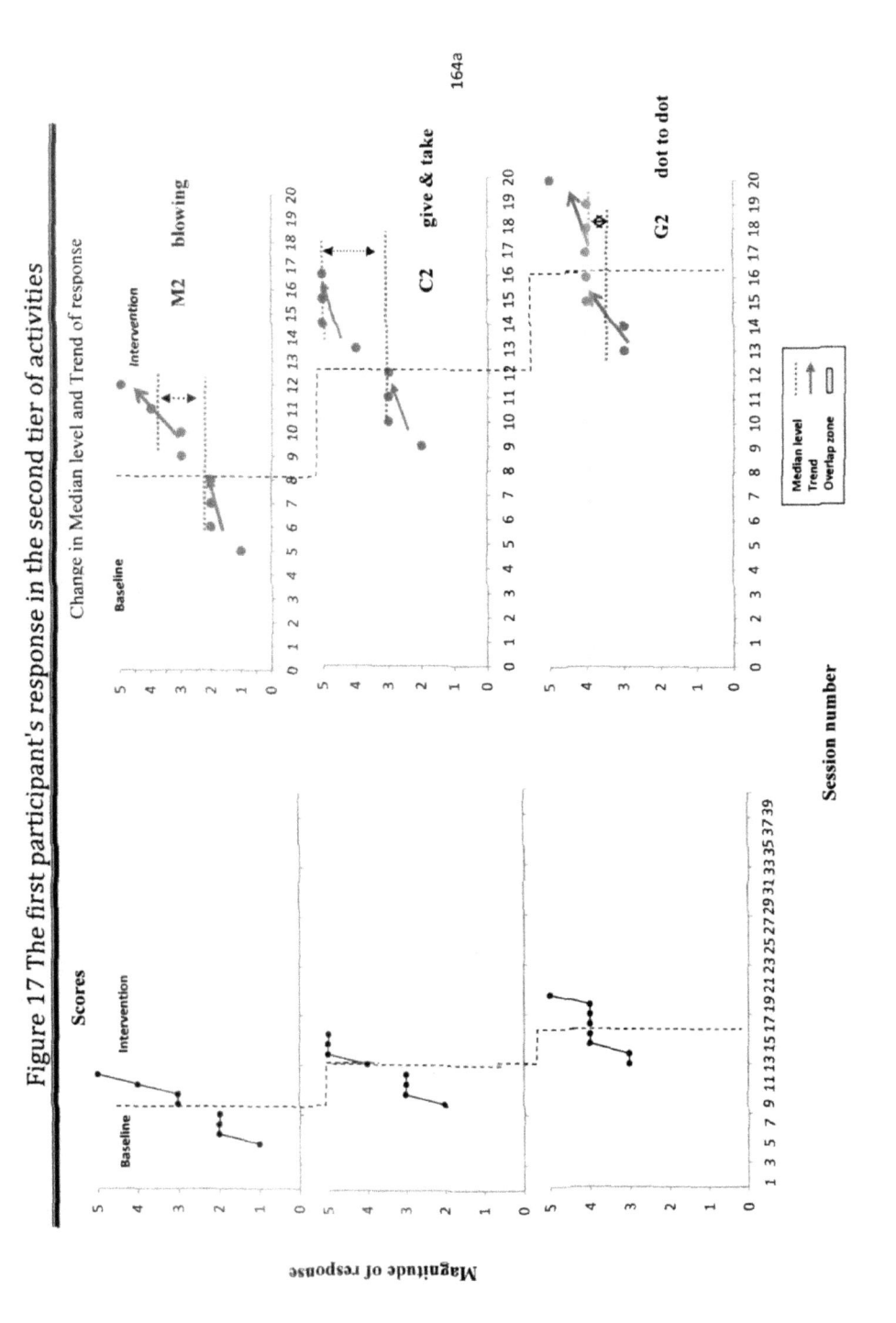

Figure 17 The first participant's response in the second tier of activities

performance significantly to five. The boy made spontaneous responses consistently across the sessions. The score showed slight variation in the baseline as well as the intervention phase. However, the trend shows an improvement in response pattern.

G2 - Dot to dot joining: The scores improved in the third session of baseline assessment. The repeated exposure must have contributed to the hike in performance. The hike is also expected to be the generalization of positive effect of the intervention in scribbling (G1) in the same session, which is a correlated task. After the phase change, also slight change was noticed in the performance. However, in the 20th session, the boy spontaneously joined two dots in a vertical stroke carefully. The median level performance shows a hike of 0.5 (From 3.5 to 4).

Effect Size

Here M2 and C2 had no values in the B phase, which overlapped. The extent to which data in the baseline versus intervention phases do not overlap is an accepted indicator of the amount of performance change. Therefore, the effect size calculated shows overall improvement in performance with the intervention. We can be 90% certain that the true effect size lies somewhere between .288 and 1.7 for M2 and for C2.

In G2 there is overlapping of scores in the intervention phase. NAP is calculated as .81, which shows medium effectiveness of the method and effect size lies between -.087 and 1.337. The interval includes zero, showing that the parameter may also be zero if repeated.

4.2.1.1.3 Third tier of activities: M3C3G3

Figure 18 illustrates the line graph showing first participant's response in the third tier.

Table 10 details the distribution of scores of the first participant for the third tier of activities.

M3 - Tongue movement: Aman used to keep his tongue retracted in the baseline phase. The median level of response improved by one point after the phase change. (From 3 to 4) Aman started protruding tongue on verbal command. The scores did not make variation within either phase.

C3 - Imitate sequence: Aman's performance varied in the baseline and the Intervention sessions. History effects were obvious, because when intervened, though he had done the sequence of actions independently, Aman got irritated with the prompting given for Sipping (M5) in the nineteenth session, which affected his performance with the subsequent activities. Initially he declined doing the task C3. When presented after other tasks he complied with physical prompts. Variability of the scores has occurred resulting in a steep downward trend. Still the medians of levels of performance in either phase shows a hike of one point (3.5 to 4.5).

G3 - Pegboard: Baseline performance was stable showing passive attempts made with verbal prompting. After the phase change, the median of performance level improved by one point (3 to 4). The score showed a variation in the 24th session. Since the boy demonstrated a better performance in another task the same day (Sipping), the subjective state of mind must have influenced the pegboard tasks also.

Effect Size

In M3 and G3 no scores overlapped after the phase change which clearly indicates performance change in the child. Therefore, the Multisensory stimulation has caused a total improvement in performance. It can be stated with 90% certainty that the effect size falls within .288 and 1.7.

In C3 there is overlapping of scores in the intervention phase. NAP is calculated as .75, which indicated the method was having medium effectiveness and the true value falls within

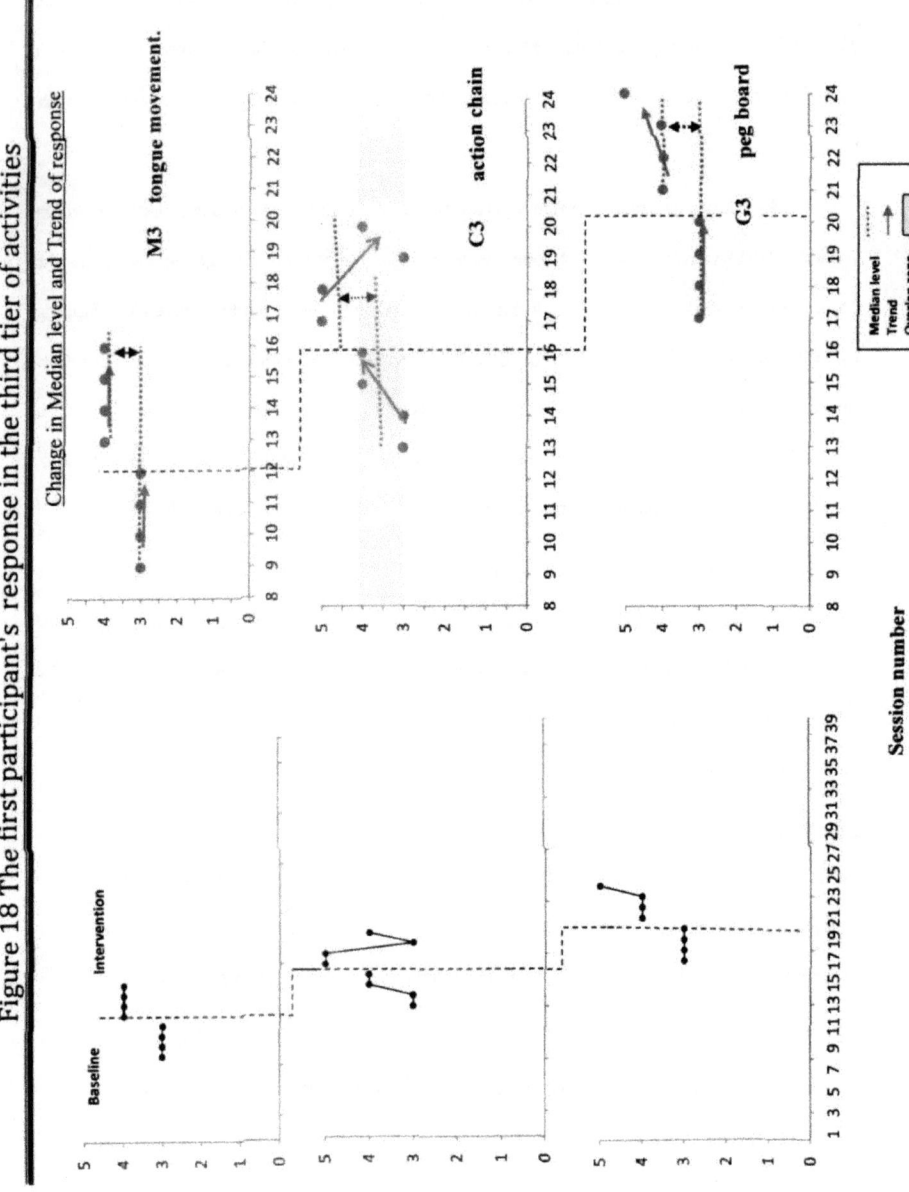

Figure 18 The first participant's response in the third tier of activities

-.212 and 1.212 which shows that the true value may also be zero.

Table 10. The distribution of scores of the first participant for the third tier of activities.

Session no.		9	10	11	12	13	14	15	16	17	18	19	20	21	22	23	24
M3	Score	3	3	3	3	4	4	4	4								
	Trend	3 to 3				4 to 4											
	Median (Level)	3				4											
	NAP				1					90% CI = .288< > 1.7							
C3	Score					3	3	4	4	5	5	3	4				
	Trend					3 to 4				5 to 3.5							
	Median (Level)					3.5				4.5							
	NAP				.75					90% CI = -.212< > 1.212							
G3	Score									3	3	3	3	4	4	4	5
	Trend									3 to 3				4 to 4.5			
	Median (Level)									3				4			
	NAP				1					90% CI = .288< > 1.7							

4.2.1.1.4 Fourth tier of activities: M4C4G4

Figure 19 illustrates the line graph showing first participant's response in the fourth tier.

Table 11 details the distribution of scores for the fourth tier of activities.

M4 - Gum movement: Baseline level was 2.5 which shifted to four in the intervention phase. This shows that the boy made gum movements on verbal prompting. Aman's score dipped by one point in the second session of the intervention phase, again due to an extraneous event in the child's environment. He got irritated when the prompting was given in the 18th session.

C4 - Response to call: the baseline score was consistently two, which improved by two points and reached four in the intervention phase. The scores showed no variation. Aman learned to respond to his name being called with verbal prompt.

G4 - Draw in different directions: Aman made active responses with physical prompts. He scored three consistently in the baseline. After the phase change, the scores made a progressive trend. By the 24th session, he made spontaneous response to directional strokes.

Figure 19 The first participant's response in the Fourth tier of Activities

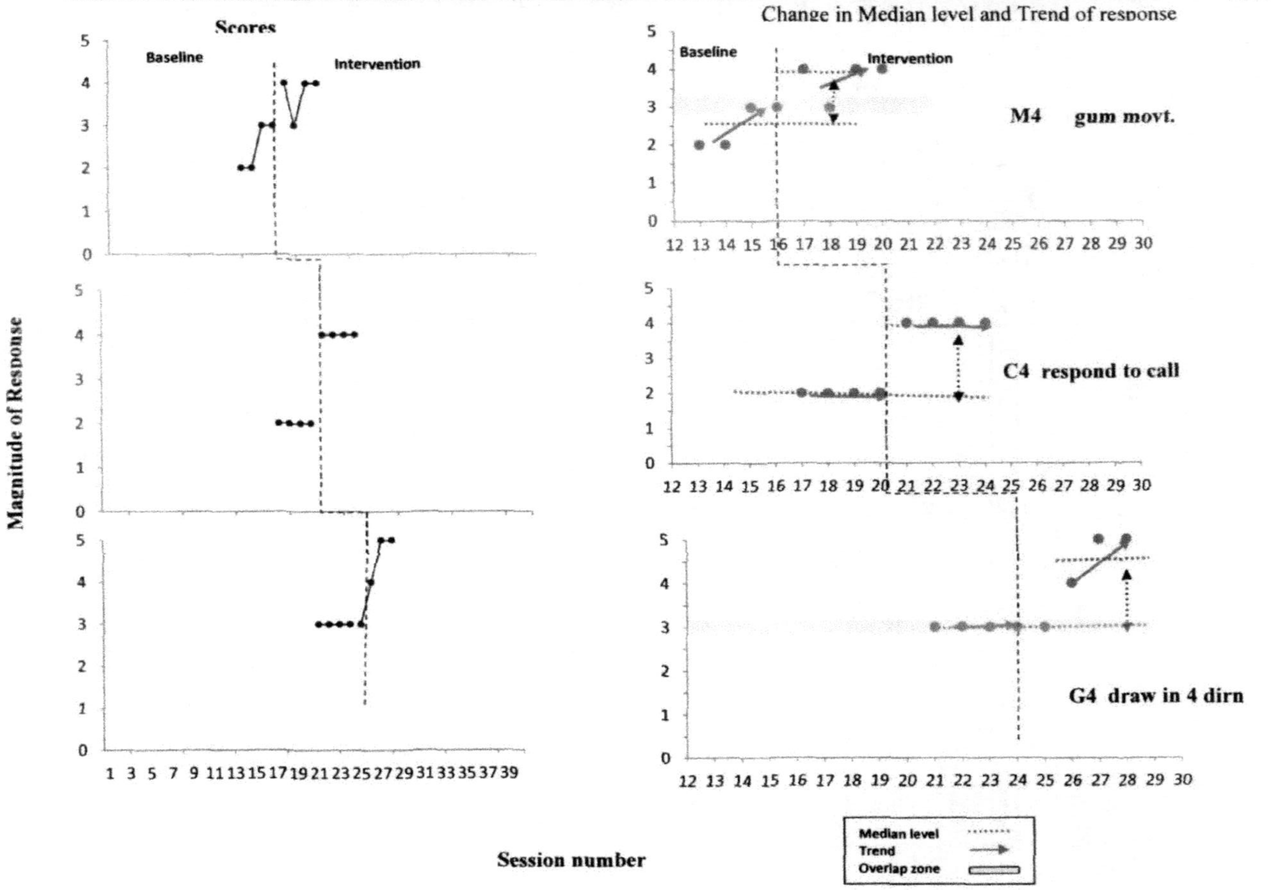

Table 11 The distribution of scores for the fourth tier of activities.

Session no.		13	14	15	16	17	18	19	20	21	22	23	24	25	26	27	28
M4	Score	2	2	3	3	4	3	4	4								
	Trend	2 to 3				3.5 to 4											
	Median (Level)	2.5				4											
	NAP	.94								90% CI = .163< > 1.587							
C4	Score					2	2	2	2	4	4	4	4				
	Trend					2 to 2				4 to 4							
	Median (Level)					2				4							
	NAP				1					90% CI = .288< > 1.7							
G4	Score									3	3	3	3	3	4	5	5
	Trend									3 to 3				3.5 to 5			
	Median (Level)									3				4.5			
	NAP				.875					90% CI = .038< > 1.462							

Effect Size

Here M4 and G4 had overlapping of scores in the intervention phase. NAP is calculated as .94 for M4 and .875 for G4, which shows a large effect. The confidence interval for true effect size of M4 is .163 to 1.58 and for G4 is .038 to 1.462. For C4 no values in the B phase overlapped which indicates a total performance change. The confidence interval for true effect size is estimated to lie within .038 and 1.462.

4.2.1.1.5 Fifth tier of activities: M5C5G5

Figure 20 illustrates the line graph showing first participant's response in the fifth tier.

Table 12 details the distribution of scores of the first participant for the fifth tier of activities.

M5 - Sipping: The baseline level of performance showed stable trend. After the phase change, the level of performance raised up to four. The scores showed a gradual hike from three to five with intervention.

C5 - Identify people: Aman made active attempts with physical prompting, throughout the baseline level observation. With intervention the score improved by one point. The scores did not show any variability within intervention phase. Aman was making appropriate response with verbal prompt with intervention.

G5 - Draw shapes: Drawing also elicited a consistent pattern of response with physical prompting. The score showed a median level of three, which improved to four in the intervention phase.

Table 12 The distribution of scores of the first participant for the fifth tier of activities.

Session no.		17	18	19	20	21	22	23	24	25	26	27	28	29	30	31	32
M5	Score	1	1	1	1	3	4	4	5								
	Trend	1 to 1				3.5 to 4.5											
	Median (Level)	1				4											
	NAP				1					90% CI = .288<>1.7							
C5	Score					3	3	3	3	4	4	4	4				
	Trend					3 to 3				4 to 4							
	Median (Level)					3				4							
	NAP				1					90% CI = .288<>1.7							
G5	Score									3	3	3	3	4	4	4	4
	Trend									3 to 3				4 to 4			
	Median (Level)									3				4			
	NAP				1					90% CI = .288<>1.7							

Effect Size

For the entire tier no values in the intervention phase overlapped indicating the effect size is 1 suggesting an absolute change in performance. The interval for true effect size is identified to be .288 to 1.7.

4.2.1.1.6 Sixth tier of activities: M6C6G6

Figure 21 illustrates the line graph showing first participant's response in the sixth tier.

Figure 20 The first participant's response in the fifth tier of activities

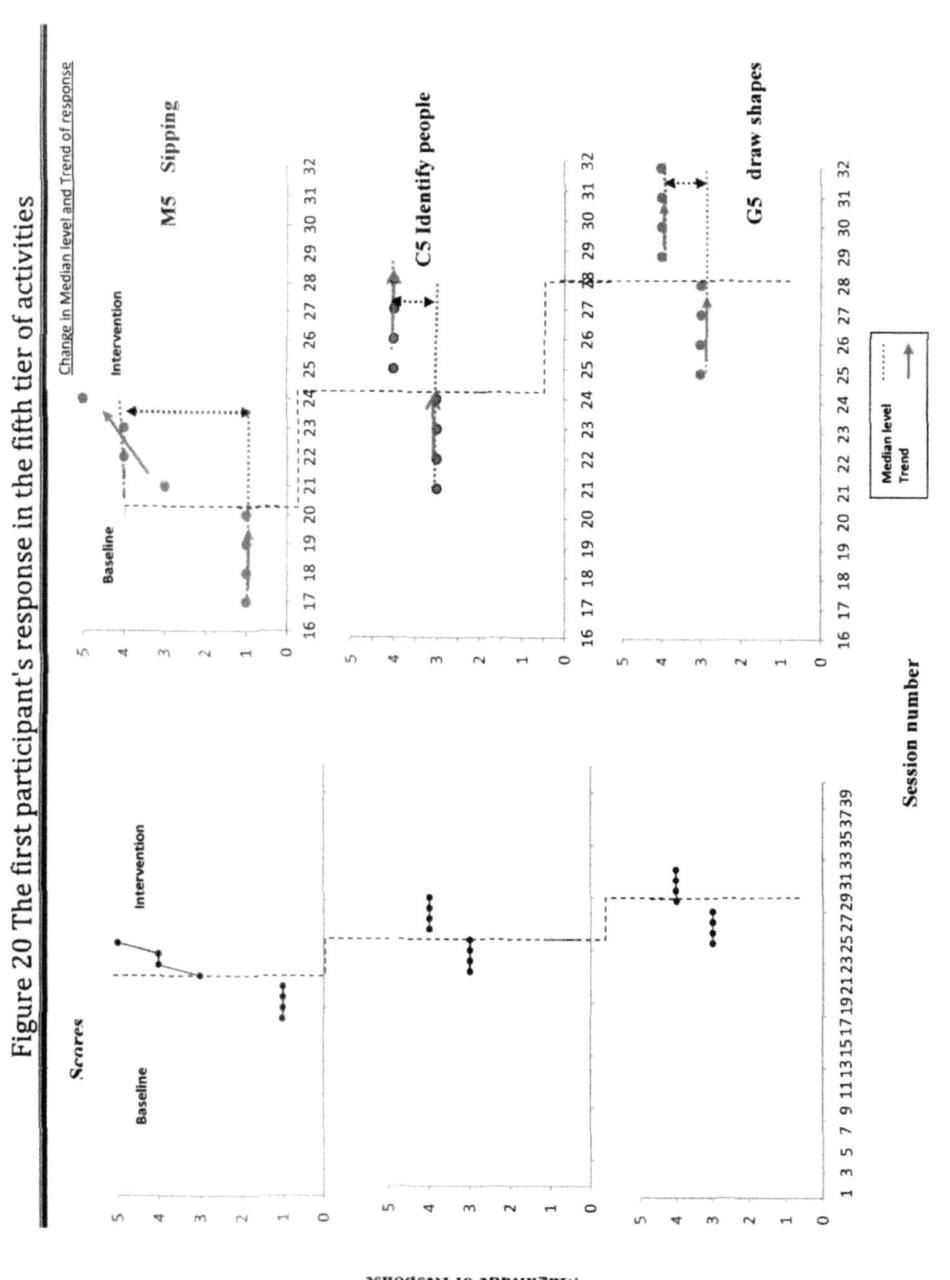

Table 13 details the distribution of scores for the sixth tier of activities.

M6 - Deep breathing: Performance of Aman varied after two sessions of baseline. The score varied from two to three after the 22nd session. The scores showed an upward trend. After the phase change, the median level of performance improved to four. The intervention scores however, did not show any variation. It is assumed the relationship between the affective and sense experience provided the basis for associative learning thereby improving his performance in the baseline of the task.

C6 - Whose? Possession: Aman made passive attempts in the baseline level itself with physical prompting. His median level of performance was two. The performance was stable in the baseline, which varied greatly with intervention. The median level went up to four point five showing significant improvement in the task. By the 31st session Aman could identify the task- whose hand is this?. He was making spontaneous responses in the last two sessions.

G6 - Picture Identification: Aman consistently scored three in the baseline level. He made no variability in response pattern. After the phase change, it slightly went up by one point and he showed appropriate response with verbal prompt.

Effect Size

Here M6 and C6 had no values in the intervention phase, which overlapped. Therefore, it is estimated that the intervention has caused an entire improvement in performance. Confidence interval for true effect size is estimated to be .288 to 1.7. In G6 there is overlapping of scores in the intervention phase. NAP is calculated as .87, which indicates a large effect. The interval for true value is estimated to be .038 to 1.462.

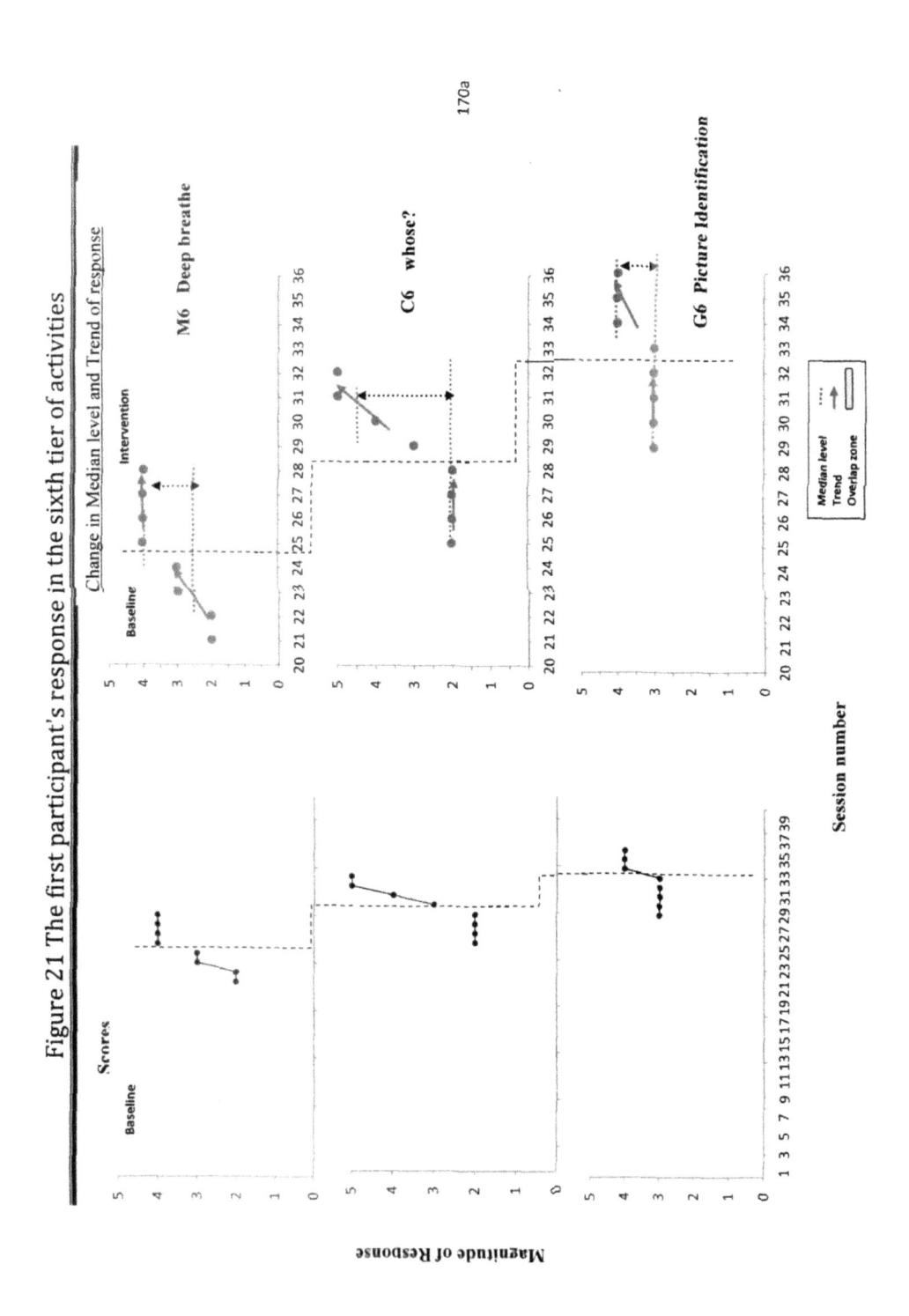

Figure 21 The first participant's response in the sixth tier of activities

M6 Deep breathe

C6 whose?

G6 Picture Identification

Table 13 The distribution of scores of the first participant for the sixth tier of activities.

Session no.		21	22	23	24	25	26	27	28	29	30	31	32	33	34	35	36
M6	Score	2	2	3	3	4	4	4	4								
	Trend	2 to 3				4 to 4											
	Median (Level)	2.5				4											
	NAP				1					90% CI = .288 < > 1.7							
C6	Score					2	2	2	2	3	4	5	5				
	Trend					2 to 2				3.5 to 5							
	Median (Level)					2				4.5							
	NAP				1					90% CI = .288 < > 1.7							
G6	Score									3	3	3	3	3	4	4	4
	Trend									3 to 3				3.5 to 4			
	Median (Level)									3				4			
	NAP				.875					90% CI = .038 < > 1.462							

4.2.1.1.7 Seventh tier of activities: M7C7G7

Figure 22 illustrates the line graph showing first participant's response in the seventh tier.

Table 14 details the distribution of scores for the seventh tier of activities.

M7 - Descend one-step per tread: Aman had a baseline score of one. The score did not vary for the four sessions. With the intervention, the scores went up by two points. The median level of performance in the intervention phase was three, the scores varied slightly, showing improvement by the 32nd session.

C7 - Yes/ No gesture: Aman did not make the gesture in the baseline sessions. The scores showed no variability. After the phase change, the median level improved to 2.5. Even though it is not revealed in the split middle trend, the scores made a cyclic trend as seen in the graph. History effects had its play; the boy was having some physical discomfort during the third session of intervention and it was reflected in the lowered performance.

Table 14 The distribution of scores for the seventh tier of activities.

Figure 22 The first participant's response in the seventh tier of activities

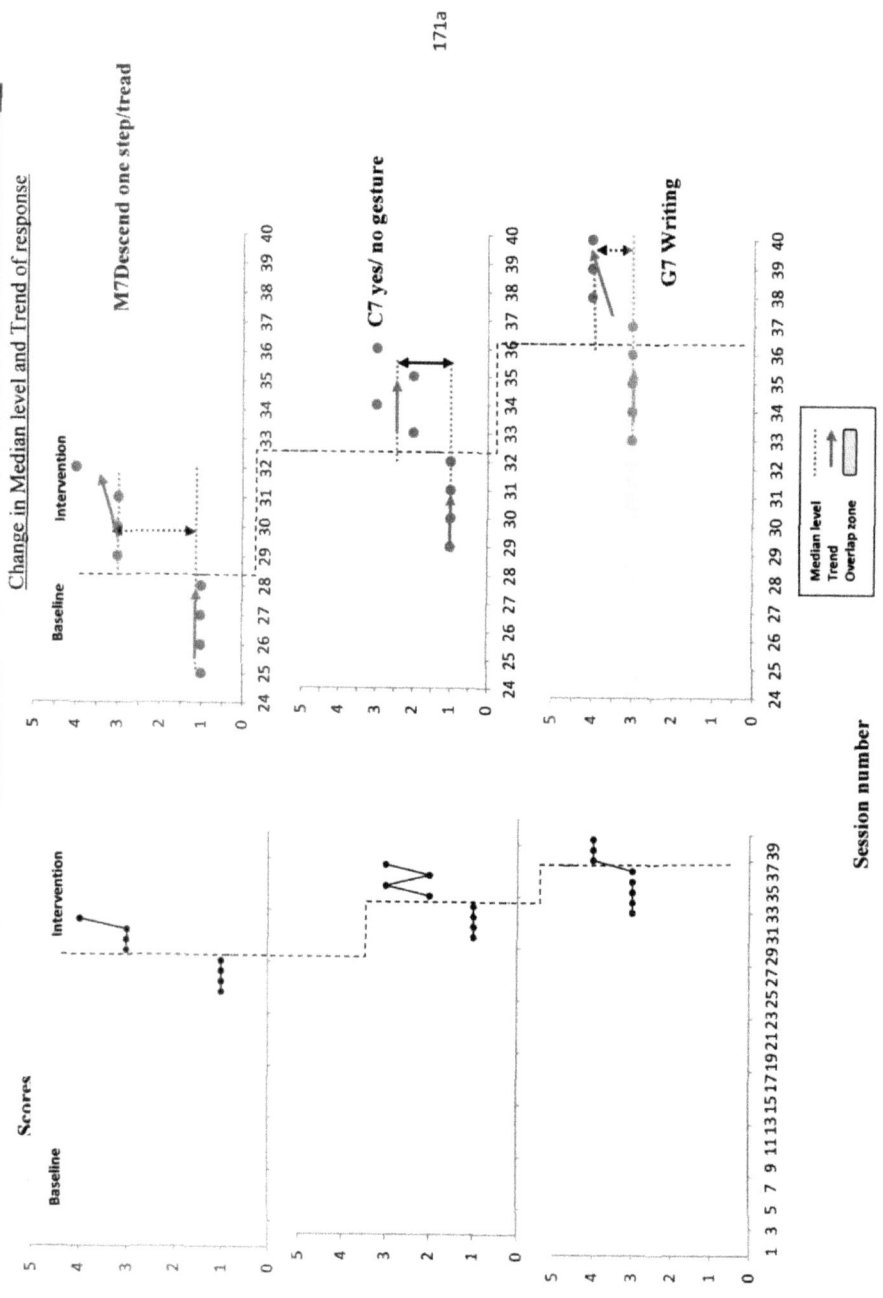

Session no.		25	26	27	28	29	30	31	32	33	34	35	36	37	38	39	40
M7	Score	1	1	1	1	3	3	3	4								
	Trend		1 to 1			3 to 3.5											
	Median (Level)		1				3										
	NAP					1				90% CI = .288<>1.7							
C7	Score					1	1	1	1	2	3	2	3				
	Trend					1 to 1				2.5 to 2.5							
	Median (Level)					1				2.5							
	NAP					1				90% CI = .288<>1.7							
G7	Score									3	3	3	3	3	4	4	4
	Trend									3 to 3				3.5 to 4			
	Median (Level)									3				4			
	NAP				.875					90% CI = .038<>1.462							

G7 - Writing: Aman made active attempts with physical prompting in the baseline sessions. The median level was three and it did not show variability. When intervened, the median level of performance went up by one point. The score made a slight progress and an upward trend.

Effect Size

In M7 and C7, no values in the intervention phase overlapped the baseline. Therefore, it is estimated that the intervention has caused a whole improvement in performance. Confidence interval for true effect size is estimated to be .288 to 1.7 for M7 and C7.

In G7, one value overlapped making NAP value .87, which nevertheless indicates a large effect. The confidence interval for true value of effect size lies between .038 and 1.462.

4.2.1.1.8 Domain wise effect of intervention for the first participant

The domain wise interpretation of the effectiveness of the intervention, the level variation and the trend variation across phases in the performance of first participant is entered on the Table 15.

Table 15 Domain wise effect of intervention for the first participant

Domain	Activity		Effect size	Level variation across phases	Trend Baseline	Trend Intervention
Motor	M1	Jumping	1	Increased	Stable	Increasing
	M2	Blowing	1	Increased	Increasing	Increasing
	M3	Tongue Movt.	1	Increased	Stable	Stable
	M4	Gum Movt.	.94	Increased	Increasing	Increasing
	M5	Sipping	1	Increased	Stable	Increasing
	M6	Deep Breathing	1	Increased	Increasing	Stable
	M7	Descend	1	Increased	Stable	Increasing
Commu Nicative	C1	Hello/Handshke	1	Increased	Stable	Stable
	C2	Give & Take	1	Increased	Increasing	Increasing
	C3	Imitate Sequence	.75	Increased	Increasing	Decreasing
	C4	Respond To Call	1	Increased	Stable	Stable
	C5	Identify People	1	Increased	Stable	Stable
	C6	Whose ?	1	Increased	Stable	Increasing
	C7	Yes/ No Gesture	1	Increased	Stable	Stable
Cognitive	G1	Scribbling	.97	Increased	Increasing	Increasing
	G2	Dot To Dot	.81	Increased	Increasing	Increasing
	G3	Peg Board	1	Increased	Stable	Increasing
	G4	Draw In 4 Dirns	.87	Increased	Stable	Increasing
	G5	Draw Shapes	1	Increased	Stable	Stable
	G6	Picture Identificatn	.87	Increased	Stable	Increasing
	G7	Writing Alphabet	.87	Increased	Stable	Increasing
	Averaging the effect size		.95			

Motor skill training:

The first participant was reportedly very passive unless encouraged. He was clumsy and awkward in movement for which he needed assistance; otherwise, he would resist participating. He would withdraw if anybody (other than the familiar / preferred persons) went closer and intruded into his large personal space. He showed mild self-stimulation in the form of rocking back and forth or flapping hands, mostly when auditory stimulations were aversive to him.

The gross motor tasks for intervention were deep pressure activities- jumping and ascending/ descending stairs with one-step per tread. Jumping helps one to better understand one's proprioceptive system (i.e., muscles and body awareness). It is a calming as well as an alerting activity. Producing an adaptive behavior against resistance may be the most effective means available for generating proprioceptive feedback. Activities that provide proprioceptive feedback are extending the head and upper trunk against gravity from the prone-lying position, extending weight-bearing limbs while jumping on a trampoline, or flexing arms to swing on a suspended trapeze (Ayres, 1979). A vestibular receptor, the labyrinth, also provides proprioceptive feedback. When proprioception is functioning efficiently, an individual's body position is automatically adjusted in different situations; for example, sitting properly in a chair and stepping off a curb smoothly (Ayres, 1979). It also allows individuals to manipulate objects using fine motor movements, such as writing with a pencil, using a spoon, and buttoning one's shirt (Ayres, 1979).However, many of these strategies have had minimal research done to prove their effectiveness. Once the trampoline was introduced in the therapy, the score showed drastic improvement. The otherwise sluggish boy seemed motivated. On later sessions, he showed voluntary attempts to explore the gadget.

Descending the stairs was introduced towards the end of the program: by that time, the boy was very co-operative and the therapist could build a warm relation. The key aspect is the reduction in anxiety about the task. It is about feeling the therapist's presence and proximity safe, consistent and dependable. The intervention required was only a direct tactile prompt on his corresponding foot to make him step down the stairs. The relationship built with him meant everything to his progress. The observations of Conner et al. (2012) that for anxious youth, "caregivers may act as emotion regulators" tend to support to the present study.

The child produced adaptive behaviors when the play experiences resulted in successfully meeting the "just right challenge". The child developed a sense of confidence, self-control and mastery that in turn provided meaning and satisfaction.

Csikszentmihalyi (1979) developed a model to explain intrinsic motivation or reward associated with play, which appears to explain the significance of the "just right challenge." He maintained that when challenge level of an activity matches the skill of an individual, 'flow' occurs that helps people to focus attention and to establish a feeling of control.

The other motor tasks given were for handling oral sensitivity. Aman could not chew food and had difficulty in swallowing also. He had an aversive response to food textures. In order to eat and drink independently the individual must have basic practic skills, oral and upper extremity motor skills and cognitive ability. Indeed, the ability to process tactile and proprioceptive input in the oral area is key to the development of adequate eating and drinking skills. Sensory processing dysfunction may manifest itself in many ways as the individual attempts to eat and drink: Immature eating patterns can be present as inability to close lips around a spoon and suck food from it, sipping from a glass and drooling, impaired ability to scoop food with spoons is due to poor proprioceptive feedback. These actions require tactile and proprioceptive discrimination, basic motor coordination and overall differentiation (Coley, 1978)

Oral motor exercises as blowing, licking, sipping and gum movements are techniques that do not involve speech production but are used to influence speaking abilities. Oral-motor therapy is often used as a component of feeding therapy to increase somatosensory awareness (Bahr, 2001; Lof & Watson, 2008). Activities given for Aman included blowing candles, sipping from a glass, tongue protrusion as if for licking a candy and breath control exercises.

In order to put off the flame, "Feeling the blow" on hand while holding him close and secure made him more attentive. Even though oral sensitivity made him anxious he co-operated. Across the species the presence of an attachment figure reduces the intensity of anxiety in the face of threat. Here the therapist acted as a secure base from which the child could pursue the goals, which are necessary for survival and adaptation. (Simpson & Neriya, 2010). Tongue protrusion required a candy to elicit an expected response. Chewing needed an oral motor tool and Sipping needed a transparent glass to elicit the appropriate response.

Sensory stimulation by itself is sufficient to motivate behavior. Motivation is the will to act, the will to work or the will to create. Stimulation on the other hand deals with spurring an initial effort or intensifying an already existing action. Without continuous stimulation, the original impact of the initial motivation can easily fade away. Motivation comes from within and from external sources (as reinforcements and punishments). The inner-directed part of the motivation has its roots in emotional attachment and curiosity (Keiler, 1959).

Aman got irritated and was weepy when he had to strive to make the tongue protrusion, chewing and sipping. Sensory stimulation also can have a strong and cumulative effect on the client's autonomic nervous system. Therefore, it was essential to observe the child's responses carefully. Some of the autonomic responses suggest over-arousal or make the child feel overly stressed or stimulated. Then steps are taken to reduce the stimulation and calm the child. Like the adage 'nothing succeeds like success', there is no more powerful therapeutic factor than the performance of therapeutic activities which were formerly impaired or inhibited (Korchin,1986). The success in an otherwise anxiety-arousing task can be quite exhilarating and could have increased the probability of favourable responses. A quite widely accepted generalization from experiments on levels of aspiration supports the fact that successful performance leads to an increased level of aspiration and that unsuccessful performance (failure) leads to a reduced level of aspiration (Child & Whiting, 1949). Here Aman's response pattern showed an increasing trend in the activities requiring oral motor movement, underscoring his enhanced motivation and aspiration.

Gross motor skills therefore should be concentrated on in the curriculum plan for autistics, as these are skills required to develop movement patterns for everyday living and promote better social interactions. Healthy gross motor development and motor awareness can facilitate spatial awareness (Corso, 1993) which is essential for laying the foundations for learning and overcoming the difficulties associated with letter identification and orientation or symbols on a page (Olds, 1994).

The effect size calculated for the motor tasks show that the multisensory stimulation given yielded a positive change in response, in almost all the motor tasks except gum movement, which also made a substantial variation in response pattern. The median level of performance across phases increased in all the seven tasks. All the tasks except tongue movement and deep breathing show an increasing trend, which suggests ongoing improvement in response pattern. The level of performance increased in all the activities because of the treatment.

Cognitive Skill training:

Acquiring a skill means to invent and to progress (Whiting, 1980 as cited in Stelmach & Requin, 1987). As children experience new sensations, they develop new cognitive skills, improve their processing abilities, and push the integrated whole to their subconscious mind. As development continues, children are able to process more and more external information without clutter or confusion. At this point, the cognitive base is in place for successful learning.

Not all people on the autism spectrum have cognitive or executive function (EF) problems. However, many do. The tendency to ignore executive function in autism treatment has had significant implications for those individuals on the spectrum who do have difficulties with EF (estimated to be as high as 80%). Many of these individuals do not progress well with social and communication issues without simultaneously addressing their difficulties with executive function. Unable to progress with teaching methods that do not consider their EF problems, they may be incorrectly classed as more profoundly or severely autistic or as both autistic and mentally retarded. The problem is not mental retardation or more severe autism, but autism combined with problems in executive function (Wertz, 2012). Therefore, the focus is switched on to activity stimulating cognitive function – scribbling.

Children write and read pictures, naturally and instinctively. They scribble and draw. Their brains are coded for literacy. If children are having trouble doing what their brains have evolved to do, something is wrong (Sheridan, 2002). They need a little push to get themselves moving. Music "is a more potent instrument than any other for education". Music can be a powerful force because of its capacity to energize and increase endurance. Physical and mental endurance can be enhanced by music's capacity to draw our attention away from the negative aspects of a task.

Music is a whole-brain activity (Parsons, Fox & Hodges, 1998). Both left and right sides are necessary for complete perception of rhythm (Tramo, 2001). Rhythm permeates our lives to such an extent that we rarely think about it. Therefore, rhymes were played and sung along with the scribbling task and it mobilized the attempt to scribble. The scores showed escalation in performance with each session.

The various levels of the task introduced were dot to dot joining, drawing in four directions, drawing shapes and writing an alphabet. Visual aids, direction indicators, tactile and kinesthetic cues, conjoined with rhythmic verbal prompts and the reassuring attitude of the resource person.

The effect size calculated for the cognitive tasks show that the multisensory stimulation given had a strong effect, particularly in two tasks, viz., peg board assorting and drawing shapes. Performance of all activities in the cognitive domain showed an increasing trend when intervened, except 'dot to dot joining', which elicited only a medium level effect (.90). Aman needed verbal prompts for executing the task. The boy was severely retarded which could have impeded eliciting a change in the cognitive skill, as is evident in the effect size estimates. For five activities, the scores did not vary immediately with intervention. Yet, the overall level of performance increased in all the activities because of the treatment. This finding converges with the study of Mann (2010) which showed that the cognitive skills of children with autism are not static, but change and, in most cases, improve over time. They also show that there is not one trajectory of autism.

Communicative skill training:

In the middle of each task, the researcher suddenly stopped playing her role, to see the communicative attempts by children to re - engage the adult in the activity. These interruption periods were included to see how children considered the activity to be a joint attempt. If children had formed a joint goal with the adult, and understood the commitment this entailed, they should try to persuade the adult to recommit to the joint goal when she stopped; instead of moving away from the task or attempting to perform the activity individually (Goswami, 2011). During the interruption periods, the children's predominate response was either to wait or to try to re - engage communicatively (e.g., by pointing to the apparatus or pushing me towards it).

Waiting for the child to initiate also means to let go of our usual sense of timing in social interactions. In typical social interactions, a response occurs within a few seconds. A break in the interaction that is any longer can often feel awkward. Still, trying not to initiate any social interaction is quite helpful at times. Whenever the child does initiate social interaction by making eye contact, communicating (verbally or non-verbally) or making physical contact, he was told that this is something important and his efforts were appreciated. This was done by praising him in some way or doing something that the child found interesting or funny or some physical response as a quick firm hug. This was to make the experience of initiating social interaction easy for the child so that he will be excited to do it more and more. In the current situation, communication skill was worked upon with the handshake task. However, the performance needed a verbal reassurance over the four sessions. The therapist waited with out stretched hands blocking Aman at the door until his hands raised slightly (but voluntarily) to meet the former's.

Aman had little speech, therefore the tasks listed for communication were eliciting appropriate communicative gestures for Hello, identifying People, their possession, making a response when called, showing nod and shake for 'yes' and 'no' and doing the give and take. Repeated rhythmic prompts were presented in tandem with the activities to elicit the appropriate response from Aman. For an autistic child a sense of comfort comes with the predictability of repetition. They gain confidence in knowing what to expect. Providing lots of time and opportunities for practice and repetition was resorted to by the therapist. Just as with favorite stories and rhymes, children love repetition and their brains are 'wired' to learn in this way. So while we may be fed up with the same track, the child will be building strong neural pathways and enjoying every minute (Brotherson, 2005).

Because singing and speech share many similarities, yet are accessed differently by the brain, music strategies can be an alternate way to practice functional communication. Music is also an effective means to organize speech by "chunking" phrases into predictable patterns and offering timing cues to assist in pacing. Since many early speech phrases are taught through repetition and imitation, these same phrases can be modeled through song as an initial teaching format, followed by fading of the music and the use of language in more natural settings (Lazar, 2007).

Music as a mode of intervention has yielded beneficial effects for the modification of behavioral problems (Burleson, Center & Reeves, 1989; Orr, Myles & Carlson, 1998).

Out of the seven communicative tasks, intervened six showed a totally improved response pattern except "imitation of sequence". The task yielded only a medium level of effectiveness using the treatment. The extraneous events that occurred at the time of intervention (History effects) while performing motor tasks are worth mentioning here. The boy got irritated with the oral motor task intervened in the same session and refused to perform the imitation sequence further. As the design was limited to four sessions of assessment the variation caused due to the chance factors could not be ruled out.

In general, all the seven tasks are indicative of an increased level of performance. The findings support the view that the median level of the target behaviors of the first participant increased across baseline and treatment phases of the research design when using a multi sensory stimulation program. Replicating the intervention with other clients is necessary to confirm the efficacy of multisensory techniques.

Regarding the trends displayed : all the activities showed an elevated response strength with the treatment and after that seven of the twenty one activities (almost 33%) maintained a stable pattern, thirteen of them showed an increasing trend (almost 62%) and one task showed a decreasing trend. Thus, it can be stated that the target behavior of the first participant showed trends during baseline and treatment phases of the research design when using a multi sensory stimulation program.

4.2.1.2 Participant 2 Sam

The nature of the levels and trends shown by the second participant in the motor, communicative and cognitive domains across the baseline and intervention phases is detailed in the following pages.

4.2.1.2.1 First tier of activities:M1C1G1

Figure 23 illustrates the line graph showing second participant's response in the first tier.

Table 16 details the distribution of scores for the second participant for the first tier of activities.

M1 - Give and Take: the median level of performance of baseline was two. This improved to three with intervention. The scores showed variability in either phase. In the third session, Sam was reported having stomach upset and he was showing irritation resulting in decline in performance scores. The trend shows a depression in the third session of baseline, probably due to history effects.

In the 7th session (intervention phase), he made a spontaneous appropriate response and secured five points. However, this was seldom repeated. As stated earlier the best performance of the four trials for a specific task in a session is scored. However the split middle trend line is stable. The median level of performance shows an improvement by one point in the intervention phase (from two to three).

C1 - Eye contact: Sam did not make eye contact for first two sessions. This varied by one point in the following sessions. When he showed irritation due to hurting tummy, he had been held close and soothened. The approach must have contributed to the hike in performance of the communicative task. After the phase change, however the response showed remarkable improvement. It hiked from a median level of two to four. Sam needed only a verbal prompt to look into my eyes. The response showed a stable trend.

G1 - Scribbling: Though Sam avoided the instructions initially, from the second session onwards he started making active efforts with physical prompting. He had crayons but the parents and teachers at the special school reported he had not been keen on sustained scribbling. The median level was three in the baseline. The trend was also stable. After the phase change, the scores did not make variation for three sessions. After wards it improved by one point. The trend is slightly up with median level score at three point five.

Effect Size

Here M1 and C1 had no values in the second phase of the design that shows an overlapping with the baseline phase. If baseline and intervention phases do not overlap it is accepted as an indicator of the amount of performance change. Therefore, the effect size is 1 indicating

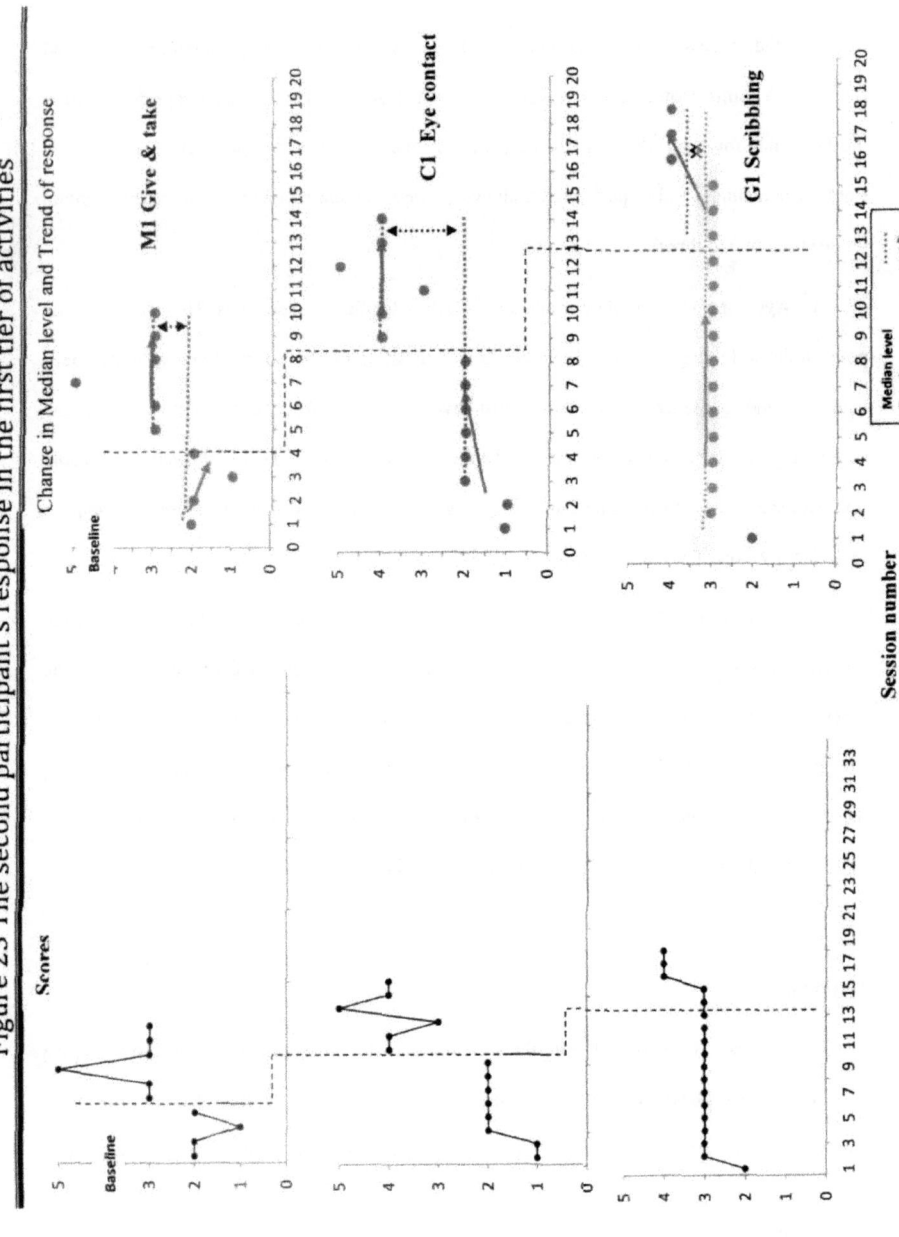

Figure 23 The second participant's response in the first tier of activities

maximum effect. The confidence interval for true effect size is .357 to 1.64 for M1 and .469 to 1.53 for C1. In G1 there is an overlapping of 3 scores. NAP is calculated as .77, which is suggestive of medium effect. The confidence interval for true effect size at 90% is .054 to 1.030.

Table 16 The distribution of scores of the second participant for the first tier of activities.

Session no.		1	2	3	4	5	6	7	8	9	10	11	12	13	14	15	16	17	18
M1	Score	2	2	1	2	3	3	5	3	3	3								
	Trend		2 to 1.5				3	to	3										
	Median (Level)		2					3											
	NAP					1						90% CI = .357< > 1.643								
C1	Score	1	1	2	2	2	2	2	2	4	4	3	5	4	4				
	Trend		1.5		to		2				4	to	4						
	Median (Level)				2							4							
	NAP				1					90% CI = .469< > 1.531									
G1	Score	2	3	3	3	3	3	3	3	3	3	3	3	3	3	3	4	4	4
	Trend			3		to		3						3		to	4		
	Median (Level)				3										3.5				
	NAP					.77						90% CI = .054< > 1.030							

4.2.1.2.2 Second tier of activities: M2C2G2

Figure 24 illustrates the line graph showing second participant's response in the second tier.

Table 17 details the distribution of scores of the second participant for the second tier of activities.

M2 - Pick and drop: Sam could not do two- step commands in the baseline level. His score did not vary. The median level of performance was one. When the performance was intervened, it markedly improved. The median level was hiked to 2.5. The scores however showed variations. Sam's response pattern showed a gradual improving trend with intervention. By the 14th session, it lowered due to hand on hand insistence. Sam could no longer find it a necessary task. He could do the pick and drop part well when asked to do. Unnecessarily prolonging the task could have resulted in the decline in response magnitude.

C2 - Hello/ handshake: Eliciting a greeting from Sam was very mechanical. He showed no response to the greeting in the baseline sessions and it improved by one point with intervention. The performance in the second phase was a stable passive one with physical prompt.

G2 - Rolling play dough: The response to the task was a stable physically prompted, passive one. This hiked by two points in the intervention phase. The scores however showed variation. The median level was four and the split middle trend shows a stable direction but the scores reveal cyclic pattern. It may be noted that Sam had problems in the tactile, vestibular, proprioceptive and visual domains and when activities pertaining to these were introduced as part of intervention, the initial resistance might have resulted in the variability of score pattern.

Effect Size

M2, C2 and G2 had a stable base line and no values in the intervention phase of the design showed no overlapping, suggesting the effect size equal to one; which is indicative of strong effect. The true effect size at 90 % confidence lies within .357 to 1.6.

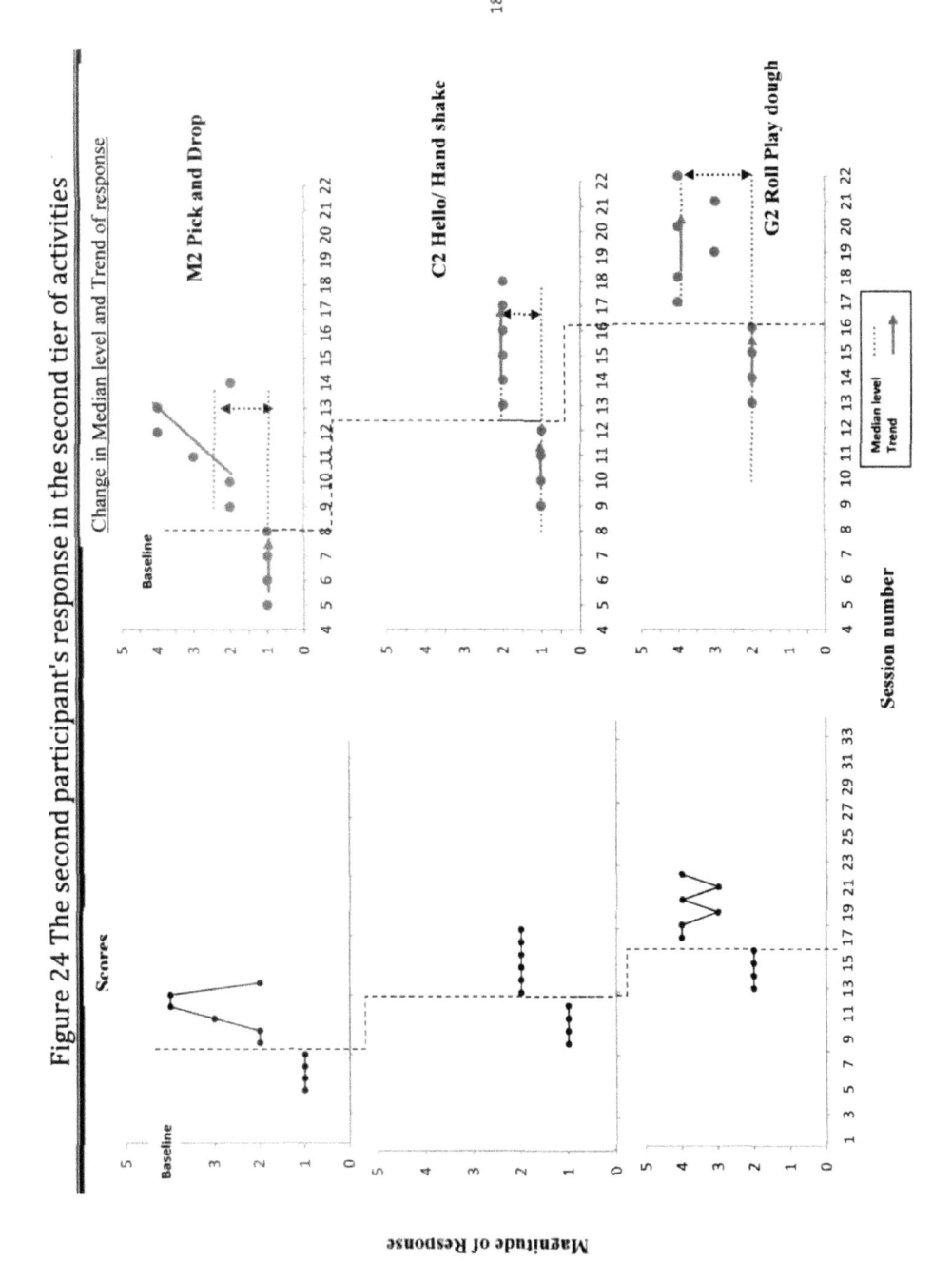

Figure 24 The second participant's response in the second tier of activities

Table 17 The distribution of scores of the second participant for the second tier of activities.

Session no.		5	6	7	8	9	10	11	12	13	14	15	16	17	18	19	20	21	22
M2	Score	1	1	1	1	2	2	3	4	4	2								
	Trend		1 to 1				2 to 4												
	Median (Level)		1				2..5												
	NAP				1					90% CI = .357 < > 1.643									
C2	Score					1	1	1	1	2	2	2	2	2	2				
	Trend						1 to 1				2 to 2								
	Median (Level)						1				2								
	NAP				1					90% CI = .357 < > 1.643									
G2	Score									2	2	2	2	4	4	3	4	3	4
	Trend										2 to 2			4		to	4		
	Median (Level)										2					4			
	NAP				1					90% CI = .357 < > 1.643									

4.2.1.2.3 Third tier of activities: M3C3G3

Figure 25 illustrates the line graph showing second participant's response in the third tier.

Table 18 details the distribution of scores of the second participant for the third tier of activities.

M3 - Jumping: Sam could not jump during the baseline sessions. His score made no variation from the minimum. After the phase change, the score improved by one point. The boy was attempting with physical prompts. It showed a stable trend.

C3 - Oral – motor movement: The baseline score was consistently 'one'. It markedly hiked up to two point five with intervention. The scores in the intervention phase showed a gradual escalation. The trend line shows a steep upward course.

G3 - Object Identification: Sam did not show signs of identification of the objects presented in the baseline sessions. However, after the phase change the response magnitude immensely changed. The median level hiked up to four. The trend line is stable in either phase, but the scores in the second phase show an initial progress, a stable level as well as a final dip. The

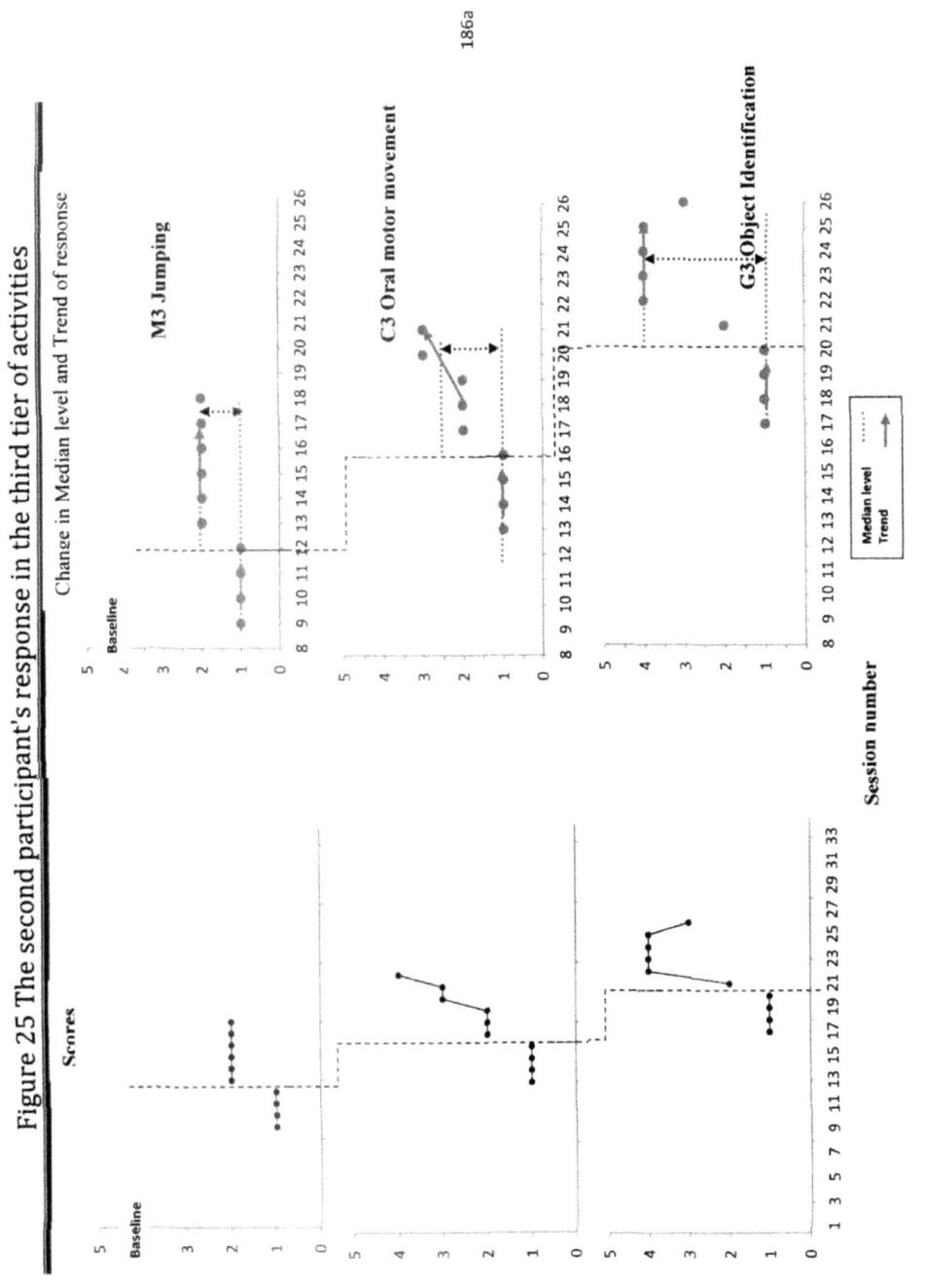

Figure 25 The second participant's response in the third tier of activities

idiosyncrasies in an autistic child's behavior repertoire was quite evident in these sessions. Sam easily gets bored of a task once he masters it. It must be his feelings of boredom or the demand for increasing the complexity of the task that he was communicating, through his complacent behavior.

Table 18 The distribution of scores of the second participant for the third tier of activities

Session no.		9	10	11	12	13	14	15	16	17	18	19	20	21	22	23	24	25	26
M3	Score	1	1	1	1	2	2	2	2	2	2								
	Trend		1	to	1		2	to	2										
	Median (Level)			1				2											
	NAP						1					90% CI = .357< > 1.643							
C3	Score					1	1	1	1	2	2	2	3	3	4				
	Trend					1	to	1			2	to	3						
	Median (Level)						1					2.5							
	NAP					1						90% CI = .357< > 1.643							
G3	Score									1	1	1	1	2	4	4	4	4	3
	Trend									1	to	1			4	to	4		
	Median (Level)										1					4			
	NAP					1						90% CI = .357< > 1.643							

Effect Size

M3, C3 and G3 had a stable base line and no values in the intervention phase made an overlap. This indicated that the intervention was highly effective. The true effect size at 90 % confidence lies within .357 to 1.6.

4.2.1.2.4 Fourth tier of activities:M4C4G4

Figure 26 illustrates the line graph showing second participant's response in the fourth tier.

Table 19 details the distribution of scores of the second participant for the fourth tier of activities.

M4 - Texture sensing: The baseline shows a variation in the score. The variation set in due to an effort made by the kid to explore the sponge ball. However, he rejected it immediately after the effort. With intervention, the median level of response tremendously improved. Sam did the task independently by the 21st session. The trend line shows a steeply upward arrow. The score show a gradual escalation from three to five.

C4 - Touch body parts: Sam's score for the task was a stable 'no response' level. After the phase change, the median level shows a significant improvement from one to four. The score showed a variation in the improving course. Trend line shows an upward course.

G4 - Pegboard: Baseline score varied when Sam tried to explore the pegs in the second session but he did not attempt in the other sessions. The median level improved significantly when intervened. After the phase change, it went up to four. The scores showed a gradual and steady upward trend.

Effect Size

Here M4 and C4 had no values in the intervention phase of the design that showed an overlap. Therefore, the effect size is 1 indicating maximum effect. The true effect size at 90 % confidence lies within .357 to 1.6.

In G4 there is overlapping of a score. NAP is calculated as .98, which indicates a strong effect. The confidence interval at 90% is found to be .315< .98 <1.6.

Figure 26 The second participant's response in the fourth tier of activities

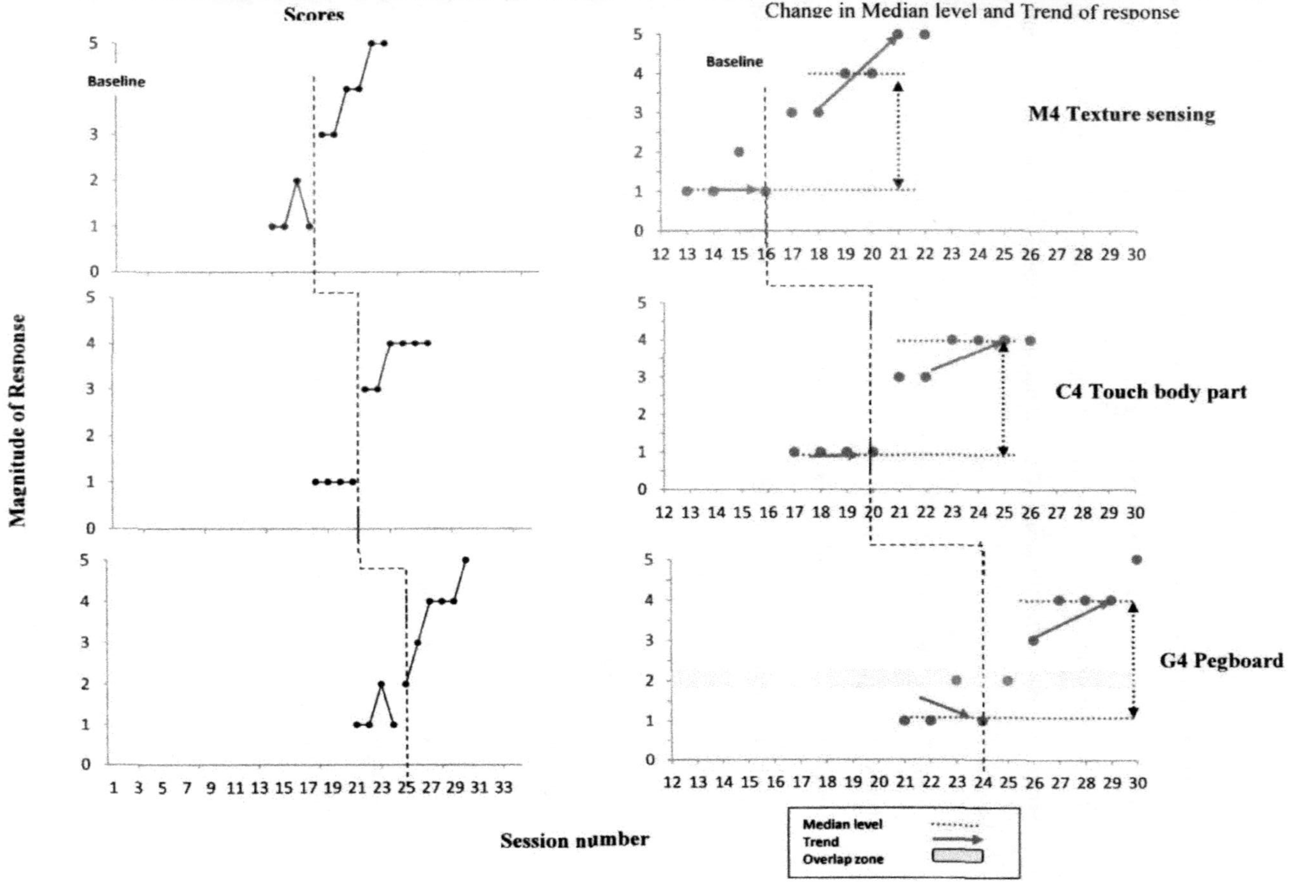

Table 19 The distribution of scores of the second participant for the fourth tier of activities

Session no.		13	14	15	16	17	18	19	20	21	22	23	24	25	26	27	28	29	30
M4	Score	1	1	2	1	3	3	4	4	5	5								
	Trend		1	to	1.5		3	to	5										
	Median (Level)			1.5				4											
	NAP					1				90% CI = .357< > 1.643									
C4	Score					1	1	1	1	3	3	4	4	4	4				
	Trend					1	to	1		3	to	4							
	Median (Level)						1				4								
	NAP					1				90% CI = .357< > 1.643									
G4	Score									1	2	1	1	2	3	4	4	4	5
	Trend									1.5	to	1			3	to	4		
	Median (Level)										1.5					4			
	NAP						.98			90% CI = .315< > 1.601									

4.2.1.2.5 Fifth tier of activities: M5C5G5

Figure 27 illustrates the line graph showing second participant's response in the fifth tier.

Table 20 details the distribution of scores of the second participant for the fifth tier of activities

    M5 - Sipping: Sam's baseline performance was "no response". After intervention, it hiked up to four, showing active attempts with a verbal prompt. The trend is stable in the first phase and it shows variation and upward trend in the second phase.

    C5 - High five: Introduction of a sign for jubilation drew his attention but the task was attempted passively with physical prompts. When intervened, the level of performance improved by two points. The trend was however stable, while the scores showed much variability,

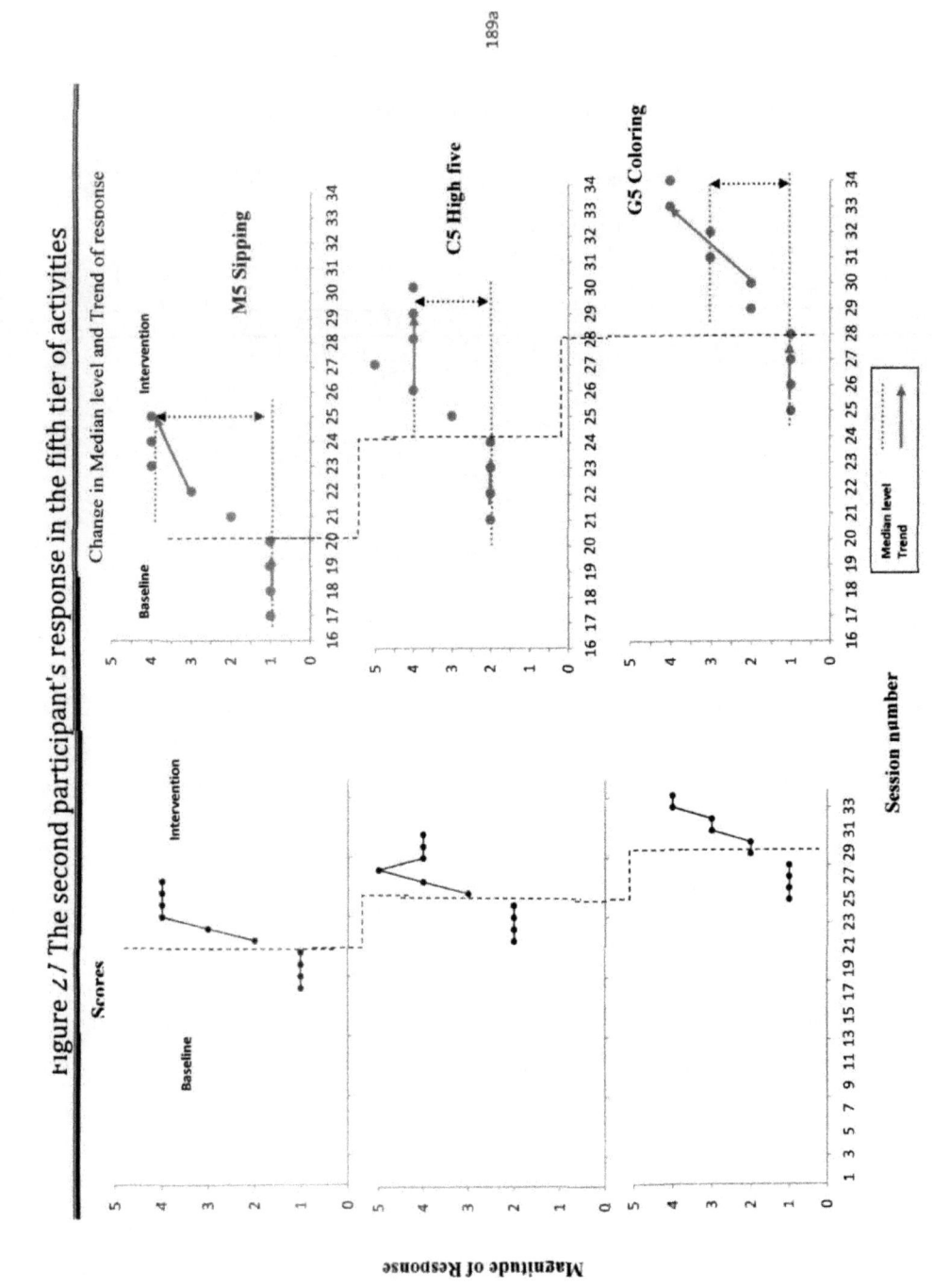

Figure 27 The second participant's response in the fifth tier of activities

probably due to history effects. In one session, the boy was so ecstatic that the response occurred quite spontaneously.

G5 - Coloring: The baseline level was stable and yielded no response in favor of the task. When intervened, the level of performance hiked by two points. The intervention scores show a stable upward trend. The scores varied steadily up in the intervention phase.

Table 20 The distribution of scores for the fifth tier of activities

Session no.		17	18	19	20	21	22	23	24	25	26	27	28	29	30	31	32	33	34
M5	Score	1	1	1	1	2	3	4	4	4	4								
	Trend		1 to 1				3	to	4										
	Median (Level)		1				4												
					1							90% CI = .357 <> 1.643							
C5	Score					2	2	2	2	3	4	5	4	4	4				
	Trend						2 to 2			4		to	4						
	Median (Level)						2					4							
						1						90% CI = .357 <> 1.643							
G5	Score									1	1	1	1	2	2	3	3	4	4
	Trend										1 to 1				2		to	4	
	Median (Level)										1					3			
						1						90% CI = .357 <> 1.643							

Effect Size

The three activities had a stable base line performance but no values in the intervention phase had an overlap with the baseline showing that the intervention was highly effective. The true effect size at 90 % confidence lies within .357 to 1.643.

4.2.1.2.6 Domain wise effect of the intervention for second participant

The domain wise interpretation of the effectiveness of the intervention, the level variation and the trend variation in the performance the second participant - Sam is entered in the Table.21

Table 21 Domain wise effect of the intervention for the second participant

Domain	Activity	Effect size	Level variation across phases	Trend Baseline	Trend Intervention
Motor	M1 Give & Take	1	Increased	Decreasing	stable
	M2 Pick & Drop	1	Increased	Stable	Increasing
	M3 Jumping	1	Increased	Stable	Stable
	M4 Texture Sensing.	1	Increased	Stable	Increasing
	M5 Sipping	1	Increased	Stable	Increasing
Commu Nicative	C1 Making EyeContact	1	Increased	Increasing	Stable
	C2 Hello/Handshake	1	Increased	Stable	Stable
	C3 Oral-Motor Movt.	1	Increased	Stable	Increasing
	C4 Identify Body Part	1	Increased	Stable	Increasing
	C5 Hit Five	1	Increased	Stable	Stable
Cognitive	G1 Scribbling	.77	Increased	Stable	Increasing
	G2 Roll Play Dough	1	Increased	Stable	Stable
	G3 Object Identifictn	1	Increased	Stable	Stable
	G4 Peg Board	.98	Increased	Decreasing	Increasing
	G5 Coloring	1	Increased	Stable	Increasing
	Averaging the effect size	.98			

Motor skill training

It is a surprising fact that many - though by no means all - autistic children are exceptionally good-looking and so was Sam. Hans Asperger, who published a pioneering account of autism in 1944, remarked on the ethereal beauty of his patients almost as if it were a diagnostic symptom. In spite of this, Sam was severely retarded and mute. His parents admitted that they do not find enough time to give the additional care required for the boy. The father comes home late and the mother kept herself busy with religious activities. The boy had high level of sensitivity in oral stimulation, bilateral co –ordination, spatial perception, emotional expression and visual motor planning as per assessment. Activities included in the domain of motor functions were intended to 'move' the child as he showed minimal interaction at school.

According to Ayres (1979), the child who is able to explore his capacity through effective interaction with the environment derives meaning and satisfaction from organizing sensations from the body and the environment and responding to them with an adaptive behavior. Meaning and satisfaction are derived from the experience of moving and interacting effectively with the environment. It is not the meaningfulness of activity per se. Finally, volition is an important prerequisite for evincing an adaptive behavior. Evincing an adaptive behavior requires effort – the kind of effort that a child gladly summons when he is emotionally involved in the task and believes he can cope with it (Ayres, 1979, p.127).

Initially Sam required a great deal of assistance until he acclimatized with the experience of being with the new person. As the child grew increasingly comfortable and competent in the new environment, the researcher gradually lessened the support and withdrew from the task at the same time remaining readily available on the periphery of the activity. The child was offered a "secure base," from which to explore and try out new activities. At the same time, monitoring was continued to watch play initiations and provide assistance whenever necessary. Although all this planning sounds as though it is very time consuming, it requires much less time than leaving the learning to chance.

Three activities fostering gross motor movements, (Give and take, pick and drop, jumping,), one focusing on somato sensory stimulation (texture sensing) and one task for oral sensitivity (sipping) were chosen.

It was taken care that the child 'does' learn to interact and is not just left to his own devices. The key is to persevere with joining in with whatever activity the child is engaged in, whether this is playing with a car or taking beads in and out of a box. Even if the child showed anger, the task was persevered, as anger is also a type of interaction and is better than no interaction at all. As this interaction is continued with Sam, he began to realize that interaction with another person could be fun.

Deep pressure touch has been found to have beneficial effects in the case of Sam. Grandin (1992) said, "At various lecture meetings of parents of autistic individuals, parents have reported to me various types of pressure-seeking behavior of their offspring, such as wrapping arms and legs in elastic bandages, sleeping under many blankets even during warm weather, and getting under mattresses. In my case, 1 used to crawl under sofa cushions and have my sister sit on them. A high functioning autistic woman stated, "I need heavy blankets on me to sleep well, or else my muscles won't calm down."

Research on autistic children indicated that they prefer proximal sensory stimulation such as touching, tasting, and smelling to distal sensory stimulation of hearing and seeing (Kootz et al. 1981). Autistic children will often seek out deep pressure sensations.

In addition, an impoverished environment, causing sensory deprivation is assumed to increase the anxiety and feelings of insecurity in the child. The family members did not seem bothered enough to alter the passive approach they held in the management of the kid. The mother had some neurological complaints and always seemed irritated in our meetings. She sat unperturbed even when the improvements in the functioning of the child was reported.

The multi sensory stimulation given included deep pressure touch stimulation as holding, swaddling, or a firm hug in addition to the gadgets presented for the activities – the trampoline, colored beads and squeeze ball.

The effect size calculated for the motor tasks show that the multisensory stimulation given yielded a positive change in response, in all the motor tasks. No scores made an overlap with the baseline. The level of performance across phases increased in all the five tasks. The bowel complaints of the kid caused a decreasing trend in performance on certain days. Apart from that, the functional level showed marked improvement day by day.

Communicative tasks training:

Krombholz (1997) stated that children who are commonly labeled as clumsy, experience tremendous difficulties in developing adequate movement skills. Poorly coordinated children perceive a lowered competence in the motor domain, have reduced social support and interaction from others, and develop higher levels of anxiety. Consequently, they are less likely to interact.

The tasks chosen for intervention were making eye contact, handshake, tongue extension, identifying body part and hit five. The exchanges of sounds and smiles between an infant and his caregiver are the first conversations, in humans. Since Sam deliberately withheld eye contact, it was chosen as the first task in the domain of communication skills. He seemed to have difficulty empathizing and seeing other's points of view, which made two-sided conversations a huge challenge for the boy. Understanding that other people may think and feel differently from oneself is one example of a child's use of "theory of mind" knowledge (Baron-Cohen, 1997). An absence of, or slowed acquisition and use of this type of theory of mind knowledge is thought to underlie some of the social impairments and deficits in empathy that is often seen in individuals with autism.

Children's confidence grows when they 'taste' success and understand that they are good at things. In the 'give and take' sessions, the praise given by the researcher built in him warmth. Everyone loves praise, and children love it most of all. So praise and encouragement was showered along with the tactics made for multi sensory stimulation.

The realization of having the ability to do something enables one to become self-directing and the individual becomes motivated to explore his capacity through the planning and production of adaptive behaviors and the participation in meaningful occupation.

The effect size estimated shows that the stimulation given for all the five tasks was effective. The scores of oral motor movement and body part identification made an increasing trend in the intervention phase while eye contact, handshake and hit five made a stable response. The level of performance increased in all the activities because of the treatment.

Cognitive skill training:

An enriched learning environment is a cornerstone of a child's brain development in infancy and childhood. The maintenance of normal, intelligent, adaptive behavior requires a continually varied sensory input. The brain must be kept warmed up and working (Bexton, Heron & Scott, 1954). Sam seemed deprived of adequate sensory stimulation from his social environment. He was not exposed to any structured and systematic pedagogic approach until then. This also could have accounted for the quick improvements noticed in the boy with the intervention.

Object identification, rolling play dough, scribbling, coloring and pegboard assorting were the cognitive tasks chosen. The activities brought in an exhilarating sense of control and independence that made the child rely solely on his own judgment. He needed time and trials for practice and repetition. The proximity of the researcher and tactile stimulation were the prime factors that triggered an enduring response from the kid.

The effect size estimated shows that the stimulation given for three tasks. Object identification, rolling play dough and coloring was very effective. The scores of scribbling and peg board assorting made some overlap but resulting an effect size estimate of .98. The level of performance increased in all the activities because of the treatment. An increasing trend in the intervention phase was seen in coloring, rolling play dough and object identification while scribbling and pegboard assorting showed a stable pattern of response.

From these, it can be concluded that the level of the target behaviors of the second participant increased across baseline and treatment phases of the research design due to multisensory stimulation. Regarding the trends displayed: all the activities indicated an elevated response strength with treatment and after that eight of the fifteen activities (almost 53%) maintained an increase in trend while seven of them showed a stable trend (almost 47%).

Thus, it can be stated that the target behavior of the second participant showed trends during baseline and treatment phases of the research design when a multi sensory stimulation procedure was used.

4.2.2 Pre-post test score comparison of the sensory profile:

The scores obtained in the various sensory domains for the four participants is entered in Table 22.

The graphical representation of the Sensory profile of first pair of children: Aman and John (noted as Participants 1 and 3)- subjected to experimental and control condition is shown in Figure 28.

4.2.2.1 Participant 1 – Aman

The scores show that the boy showed sensory problems in 15 out of the 24 indices to various extents. The change in sensitivity issues noticed as per the inventory scores is detailed in the Table 23.

As can be observed from the table, eleven of the 15 sensory problems were overcome after the three-month multisensory stimulation procedure.

There was even a reduction in two indices viz., - oral sensitivity and visual motor planning - where the score in fact dropped down from a high level to moderate. Oral sensitivity was shown in the form of spitting out or rejecting food and resistance in tooth brushing. According to the parent, the resistance in these activities showed reduction. He now permits the tasks, but at times shows irritability. Visual Motor planning problems were reported as "difficulty in ascending and descending stairs, difficulty in puzzles and writing skills". The training program had focused on the stair climbing as well as writing skills. The report from parents as well as the Occupational therapist confirmed the improvement.

However, no obvious change was noticed in the following two areas pertaining to the visual modality: in the Visual – General behavior section, he was reported to continue watching every one when they move about the room. This has not varied in the post intervention assessment either. Hence, the index remained low.

Table 77 Sensory index inventory scores of the four participants

Sensory Integration Inventory		AMAN - Expermtl		JOHN - Control		SAM - Expermtl		ROSHAN - Control	
		Pre	Post	Pre	Post	Pre	Post	Pre	Post
Tactile									
Dressing	Tactile	0	0	0	0	0	0	0	0
Oral sensitivity	Tactile	1	0.5	0.5	0.5	1	0.5	0	0
personal space	Tactile	1	0	1	1	0	0	0.5	0.5
Social behavior	Tactile	0.14	0	0	0	0.28	0.28	0.43	0.43
Self stimulatory behavior	Tactile	0	0	0	0	0	0	0	0
Self injurious behavior	Tactile	0	0	0	0	0	0	0	0
Vestibular									
Muscle tone	Vestibular	0.25	0	0	0	0.5	0.5	0.25	0.25
Equilibrium responses	Vestibular	0	0	0	0	0.6	0.6	0.6	0.6
Posture and Movement	Vestibular	0.2	0	0.2	0.2	0.6	0.3	0.9	0.9
Bilateral Co-ordination	Vestibular	0	0	0	0	1	0.6	0.3	0.3
Spatial Perception	Vestibular	0.6	0	0.3	0.3	1	0.6	1	1
Emotional expression	Vestibular	0	0	0	0	1	0.5	1	1
Self stimulatory behavior	Vestibular	0.14	0	0.43	.43	0.3	0.3	0.3	0.3
Proprioception									
Muscle tone	Proprioception	0.14	0	0.3	0.3	0.6	0.43	0.86	1
Motor skills/planning	Proprioception	0.1	0	0.1	0.3	0.6	0.3	0.5	0.5
Self stimulatory behavior	Proprioception	0.4	0	0.4	0.4	0.6	0.5	0.4	0.5
Self injurious behavior	Proprioception	0	0	0	0	0	0	0	0
Auditory									
Social behavior	Auditory	0.4	0	0.4	0.8	0.6	0.6	0.6	0.6
Self stimulatory behavior	Auditory	0	0	0.3	0.3	0	0	0	0
Visual									
General behavior/ social	Visual	0.1	0.1	0.2	0.2	0.2	0.2	0.6	0.6
Visual spatial	Visual	0.75	0.75	0.5	0.75	0.75	1	0.5	0.25
Motor planning	Visual	1	0.6	0.6	1	1	1	1	1
Self stimulatory behavior	Visual	0	0	0.5	0.5	0	0	0	0
General Reactions	General Reactn	0.3	0	0.3	0.3	0.5	0.3	0.7	0.7
Average score		.27	.08	.25	.3	.46	.35	.43	.43
Difference score (post - pre)			-.19		.5		-.11		0

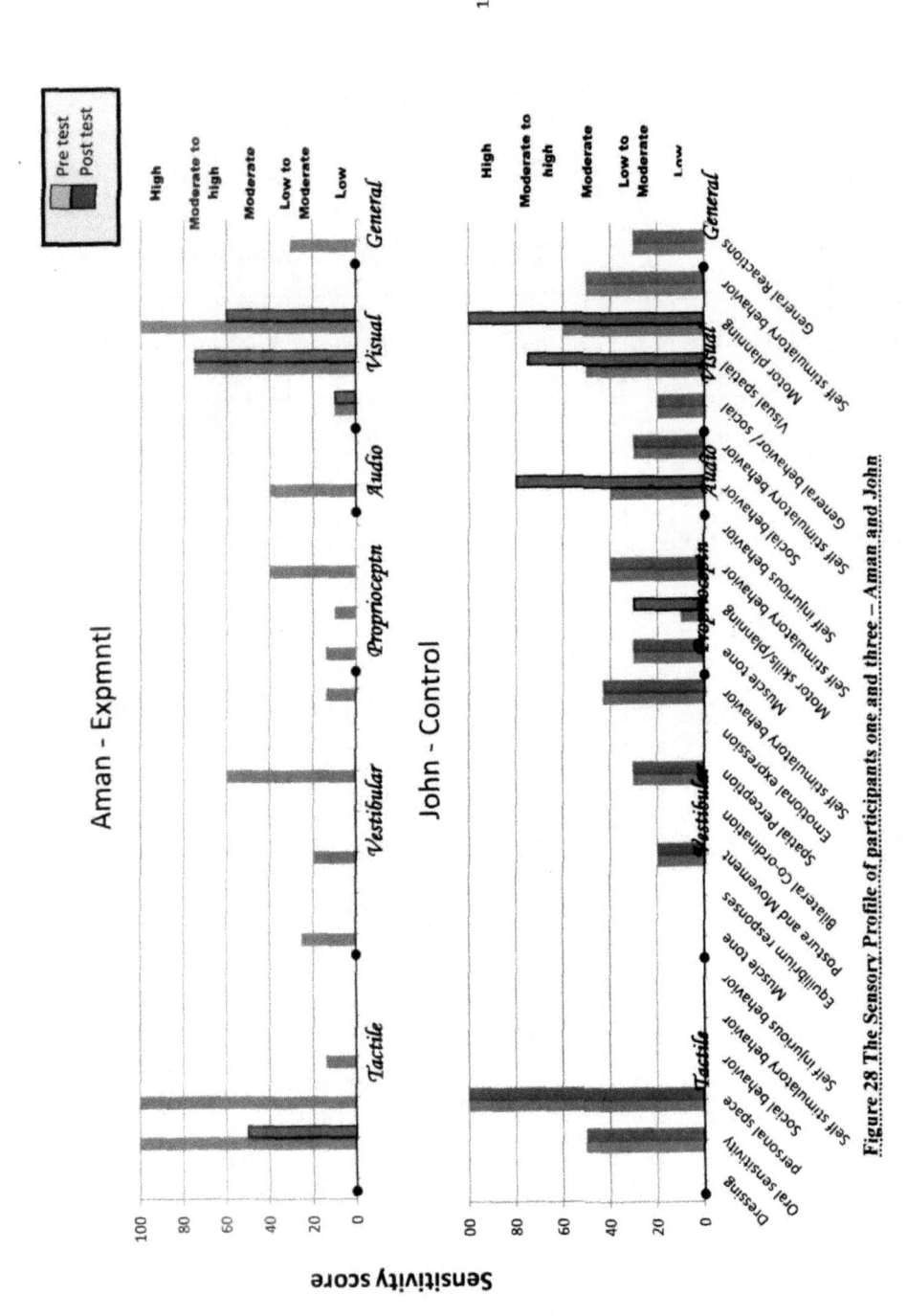

Figure 28 The Sensory Profile of participants one and three – Aman and John

Similarly, in the visuo-spatial section, it was reported that he looks carefully or intently at objects or people. He gets lost easily and has trouble staying between lines while coloring or writing. The report after intervention shows the same status. The index is suggestive of a moderate to high-level sensitivity in visual spatial tasks.

Table 23 Variation noticed in the post test scores of the sensory profile of the first participant

Sensory issue		Change noticed			
		Overcame	Reduced	No change	Hiked
Tactile	Oral sensitivity		✓		
	personal space	✓			
	Social behavior	✓			
Vestibular	Muscle tone	✓			
	Posture and Movement	✓			
	Spatial Perception	✓			
	Self stimulatory behavior	✓			
Proprioception	Muscle tone	✓			
	Motor skills/planning	✓			
	Self stimulatory behavior	✓			
Auditory	Social behavior	✓			
Visual	General behavior/ social			✓	
	Visual spatial			✓	
	Motor planning		✓		
General Reactions		✓			

4.2.2.2 Participant 3 - John

The change in sensitivity issues noticed as per the inventory scores is detailed in the Table 24.

Table 24 Variation noticed in the post test scores of the sensory profile of the third participant

Sensory issue		Change noticed			
		Overcame	Reduced	No change	Hiked
Tactile	Oral sensitivity			✓	
	personal space			✓	
Vestibular	Posture and Movement			✓	
	Spatial Perception			✓	
	Self stimulatory behavior			✓	
Proprioception	Muscle tone				✓
	Motor skills/planning			✓	
	Self stimulatory behavior				✓
Auditory	General behavior/ social				✓
	Self stimulatory behavior			✓	
Visual	General behavior/ social		.	✓	
	Visual spatial				✓
	Motor planning				✓
	Self stimulatory behavior			✓	
General Reaction				✓	

As Table 24 indicates, John, the matched pair of Aman in the controlled group showed sensitivity in 15 out of the 24 indices to various extents. Post assessments after a three-month period showed that the child's sensitivity, worsened in the following areas:

In **Auditory social behavior,** John was reported to continue responding aversively to unexpected or loud noise like mixie, cooker whistle etc and had trouble working with background noise. After three months, it was reported that he "holds hands over ears and appears not to hear what we say". The graph shows that the behavior, which used to be at a low to moderate level worsened to a moderate to high level.

The visual spatial behavior: John was reported as getting lost easily and having trouble staying between lines while coloring or writing. The report after three months showed that "he becomes frustrated when trying to find objects in competing backgrounds." The graph showed that the behavior that was at a low to moderate level initially worsened to a moderate to high level.

The Visual Motor planning problems were reported as "difficulty in ascending and descending stairs, difficulty in puzzles and writing skills". After three months, the report from parents as well as the Occupational therapist shows that his 'writing also became illegible now'. The sensitivity index scaled up to the maximum from a moderate level.

The Motor skills planning-included under the **Proprioception** also worsened. It had been at a low level and hiked to low to moderate level after three months.

No obvious change was noticed in eleven areas as seen in the Table 24.

4.2.2.3 Participant 2 - Sam

The graphical representation of the Sensory Index profile of the second pair of children: Sam and Roshan – noted as Participants 2 and 4-subjected to experimental and control condition is shown in Figure 29. The change in sensitivity issues noticed as per the inventory scores is detailed in the Table 25.

As can be observed from the table, the scores show that the boy presented problems with sensitivity in 17 out of the 24 indices to various extents. After the three-month multisensory stimulation program, improvements were noticed in the following nine areas:

Oral sensitivity has dropped down from a high level to moderate. The sensitivity was shown in the form of spitting out or rejecting food and resistance in tooth brushing. According to the parent, the resistance in eating and sipping reduced. Though he permitted tooth brushing, irritability persisted

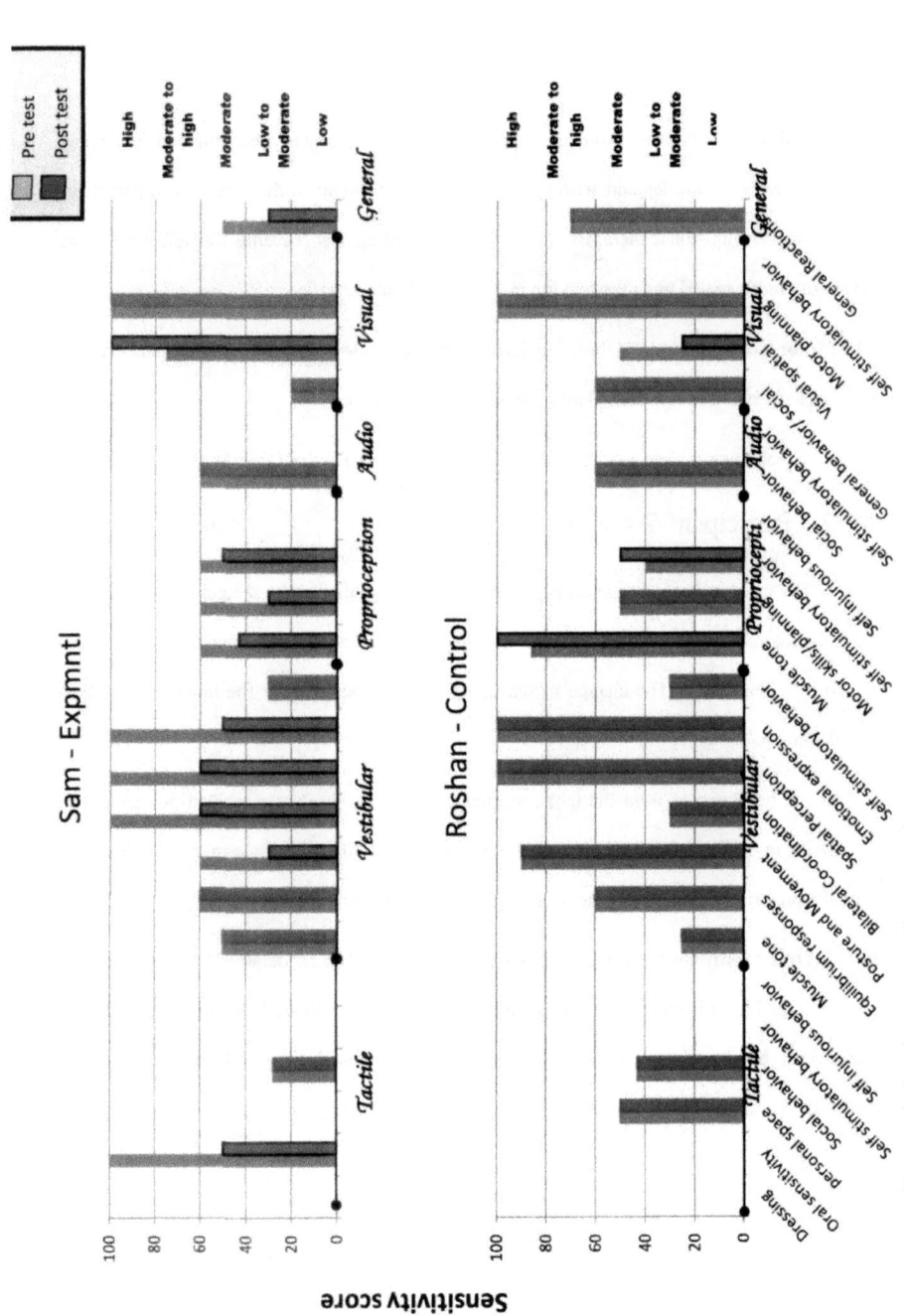

Figure 29. The Sensory Profile of participants two and four – Sam and Roshan

Table 25 Variation noticed in the post test scores of the sensory profile of the second participant

Sensory issue		Change noticed			
		Overcame	Reduced	No change	Hiked
Tactile	Oral sensitivity		✓		
	Social behavior			✓	
Vestibular	Muscle tone			✓	
	Equilibrium responses			✓	
	Posture and Movement		✓		
	Bilateral Co-ordination		✓		
	Spatial Perception		✓		
	Emotional expression		✓		
	Self stimulatory behavior			✓	
Proprioception	Muscle tone		✓		
	Motor skills/planning		✓		
	Self stimulatory behavior		✓		
Auditory	General behavior/ social			✓	
Visual	General behavior/ social			✓	
	Visual spatial				✓
	Self stimulatory behavior			✓	
General Reactions			✓		

Vestibular posture and movement: It was reported that Sam had poor heel-toe pattern, had head-neck-shoulder rigidity, and resisted being moved by others. He needed assistance with overhead reach, demonstrated poor postural background movements and resisted participating in movement activities. After three months' intervention, it was noticed that the head-neck-shoulder rigidity, resistance for movements and participating in activities have significantly reduced. The graph showed a descent from moderate level sensitivity to a low to moderate level.

Vestibular bilateral co ordination of Sam was reported as 'Using mainly one hand at a time in activities requiring two, avoids mid line crossing and uneven timing in bilateral movements. After intervention, it was reported that he has started using either hands in ball catching as well as carrying bag to school. The level has dropped from a high-level sensitivity to moderate level.

Vestibular - Spatial perception difficulties included bumping into objects, difficulty walking around furniture, difficulty going through doorways, hesitancy at stairs and difficulty in ascending and descending stairs. After intervention, it was noticed that Sam was more oriented and alert. He no more bumped into objects or had any difficulty walking around furniture. The histograms show a dip from high-level sensitivity to moderate level.

Vestibular - Emotional expression. Sam used to display gravitational insecurity, became irritable when moved, or upset at changes in room arrangement and looked anxious when moving from place to place. After the therapy, it was noticed that he was still anxious, but does not show irritability when moved from place to place. He was no more upset about the changes in the room arrangement. The figure shows a drop in level from high to moderate.

Proprioception – Muscle tone: Sam was passive unless encouraged or assisted in movement. He demonstrated a weak grip and displayed poor muscle contraction. After the intervention, it was noticed that the passivity has reduced, but the level change is not appreciable.

Proprioception –Motor skills/planning and body image: Sam does not shape hand to hold objects or another person's hand. If forced he holds objects in hand instead of manipulating it. He touches or holds objects lightly. He is clumsy or awkward in movement. He does not position self squarely on furniture or equipment. He is awkward when getting on or off equipment. After the intervention, the parents reported that the boy has shown an improved grip. He holds objects better. The score for sensitivity shows a drop from moderate level to low to moderate level.

Proprioception – Self-stimulatory behavior: Sam toe-walks. When irritated he pulls against objects, clenched his teeth and banged. He pushes or leans heavily against people or furniture.

The post intervention assessment showed that his irritability has reduced slightly. The score shows a dip but is paltry.

General reaction: Sam was slow to recover or difficult to calm when upset. He had unpredictable emotional outbursts, difficulty orienting to others' activities and delayed response to social communication. After three months of intervention, the parents reported that his irritability has reduced and it is easy to calm him down. The whining has reduced markedly. The score change is visible with a decrease in the level from moderate to low to moderate level.

Seven of the following indices showed any variation (Vide Table 25).

Tactile- Social behavior, Vestibular- muscle tone, Vestibular - equilibrium responses, Vestibular - self-stimulatory behavior, Auditory - general behavior, Visual - general behavior and Visual - self stimulatory behavior.

In one area, viz., the visuo spatial, even a hike in sensitivity was observed. It was reported that Sam becomes frustrated when trying to find objects in competing backgrounds and he has trouble staying between lines while coloring or writing. The report after intervention shows that he now looks even more carefully or intently at objects or people. Thus graph indicates an elevation from 'moderate to high level' to 'High level'.

4.2.2.4 Participant 4 - Roshan

The change in sensitivity issues noticed as per the inventory scores is detailed in the Table 26.

Table 26 Variation noticed in the post test scores of the sensory profile of the fourth participant

Sensory issue		Change noticed			
		Overcame	Reduced	No change	Hiked
Tactile	personal space			✓	
	Social behavior			✓	
Vestibular	Muscle tone			✓	
	Equilibrium responses			✓	
	Posture and Movement			✓	
	Bilateral Co-ordination			✓	
	Spatial Perception			✓	
	Emotional expression			✓	
	Self stimulatory behavior			✓	
Proprioception	Muscle tone				✓
	Motor skills/planning			✓	
	Self stimulatory behavior				✓
Auditory	General behavior/ social			✓	
Visual	General behavior/ social			✓	
	Visual spatial		✓		
	Self stimulatory behavior			✓	
General Reactions				✓	

As Table 26 indicates, the scores show that Roshan showed sensitivity in 17 out of the 24 indices to various extents.

After the three month multi sensory stimulation procedure, the following changes were noticed:

The **Visual spatial** domain showed obvious improvement. Roshan used to become frustrated when trying to find objects in competing backgrounds and he had trouble staying between lines while coloring or writing. The report after intervention showed that he colors much better now. It had been at the high level of sensitivity and dropped to low to moderate level after three months.

However two indices of **Proprioception** have shown a hike indicating that the child's sensory problem has worsened in two areas. Items assessing the muscle tone show that Roshan was now getting tired easily. His self-stimulation in the form of clapping and stamping has aggravated to an unusual degree. The muscle tone has varied slightly and the self-stimulation varied from a Low to moderate level to moderate level.

No variation was noticed in fourteen indices viz., Tactile - personal space and social behavior, Vestibular - muscle tone, equilibrium response, posture and movement, bilateral co – ordination, spatial perception, emotional expression and self-stimulation, Proprioception – motor skills/planning, Auditory - social behavior, Visual - general behavior and motor planning and General Reactions (Vide Table 26).

Discussion

The difference score calculated in the sensory index over a period of three months shows that the first participant made an improvement of almost 20 % (.19) in domains where sensitivity issues were high, compared to his matched equivalent who showed a 5% aggravation of the problem. The second participant had his sensitivity score reduced by 11% (.11) and his matched pair, the fourth participant, had no change at all noticed in three months. The data indicates that the intervention was successful in creating a notable change in the Sensory profile of the experimental group, when compared against the control group. However, the study needs to be replicated with other subjects before generalizing the results.

Too much data force the researcher to focus on the area in which the experimental subjects show improvement, as it advocates the efficacy of the intervention technique. Active participation of the individual in treatment has obvious implications, that is passive movement imposed by external forces does not have the same effect on proprioceptors as does active movement (Evarts, 1985; Kalaska, 1988). When joint movement is active, it is hypothesized that an efferent copy (corollary discharge) of a centrally generated motor command is sent to sensory centers in the brain for comparison to the reference of correctness. When movement is passively imposed, no motor command is generated and no efferent copy is sent to sensory centers (Matthews, 1988). Vestibular- proprioceptive feedback from movements contributes to the development of neuronal models or the memory of how it feels to perform a given movement. According to Brooks (1986), this information is used in two ways: it regulates ongoing present activity and it guides as part of the motor memory, the execution of such a task in future. Thus, our sense of effort and its memory are essential to both the execution and planning of motor action.

Here, the focus was on improving active participation of the subjects, which must have contributed to the significant variation in the vestibular – proprioceptive issues of the two experimental subjects. Eliciting an adaptive behavior against resistance through the use of a trampoline is the most effective means available for generating proprioceptive feedback.

Deep touch-pressure and proprioceptive information can modulate arousal. The researcher reassured the children with the deep touch pressure whenever there was an anxiety-arousing situation, probably contributing to the reduction in tactile sensitivity. Farber (1989) supported a beneficial response to the application of deep pressure, suggesting that maintained pressure is calming as it facilitates an increase in parasympathetic or relaxed tone. In describing her own autism, Temple Grandin related her experience of severe anxiety and how deep pressure ultimately helped her reduce the anxiety's debilitating effects by reducing overall arousal and facilitating attention and awareness (Grandin & Scariano, 1986). In studies done with children with autism, deep pressure has been found to have a calming effect. (Vanden Berg, 2001).

The oral motor tasks given has brought about salient changes in the sensitivity of either child subjected for intervention.

The summary, major findings of the study, and suggestions for future research are presented in the next chapter.

5. SUMMARY, FINDINGS AND SUGGESTIONS

5.1 Study in Retrospect

5.2 Major Findings

5.3 Tenability of Hypotheses

5.4 Implications of the study

5.5 Limitations of the Study

5.6 Suggestions for Further Research

5.1 Study In Retrospect

5.1.1 Restatement of the Problem

The purpose of this study was to examine the effectiveness of a Multisensory stimulation procedure in the management of two children with autism.

5.1.2 Variables of the Study

The study was designed with the following two sets of variables:-

(1) **Dependent Variables**: The study included three dependent variables:

motor skills, communicative skills and cognitive skills of the subject

(2) **Independent Variable**: The multisensory stimulation procedure designed according to the sensory profile of each child.

5.1.3 The Research question and the hypotheses

The central research question was;

- Does the use of Multi sensory stimulation procedure prove effective in the management of autism?

The hypotheses formulated for the study were:

1. There is significant difference between the scores assigned by the researcher and the observer for the performance of the first participant in the behavior modification program focusing on multisensory stimulation procedure.

2. There is significant difference between the scores assigned by the researcher and the observer for the performance of the second participant in the behavior modification program focusing on multi sensory stimulation procedure.

3. The level of the target behavior of the first participant varies across baseline and treatment phases of the research design when using a multi sensory stimulation procedure.

4. The level of the target behavior of the second participant varies across baseline and treatment phases of the research design when using a multi sensory stimulation procedure.

5. The target behaviors of the first participant show trends during baseline and treatment phases of the research design when using a multi sensory stimulation procedure.

6. The target behaviors of the second participant show trends during baseline and treatment phases of the research design when using a multi sensory stimulation procedure.

7. There will be substantial difference in the sensory profile of the experimental group, after Multi sensory stimulation procedure when compared against the control group.

5.1.4 Method

The methodology used for the study is briefly described as follows:

5.1.4.1 Sample for the Study

Two children, one moderately autistic and the other severely autistic were chosen for the intervention program. A control group of matched pairs is also selected for pre post temporal comparison of sensory profile variation.

5.1.4.2 Tools used for measurement

The following four tools were used by the investigator for the purpose of the study.

5. **Vineland's Social Maturity Scale** (Malin,1992). VSMS gives an index of the child's social and adaptive development and yields a Social Quotient (SQ).

6. **Childhood Autism Rating Scale (CARS)** (Schopler, Reichler, & Renner, 1999), distinguishes children with autism in the mild/moderate/severe range.

7. **The Sensory Integration Inventory** (Reisman & Hanschu, 1992) The Sensory Integration Inventory-Revised(SII-R) is used to screen and rule out serious maladaptive behaviors that are not due to sensory dysfunction. For the comparison of profiles, the scores are entered as percentage of sensitivity in each area.

8. **Curriculum Guide for Autistic Children** (Maurice,1996) The module provides a chronological pattern of activities that could be introduced and worked out on children with developmental disabilities. Those activities that the child could not perform were chosen as the tasks to be intervened.

Besides, data about the history and current functional status of the subjects were collected by the researcher with assistance from the special educator, psychologist, speech pathologist and occupational therapist.

5.1.4.3 Design of the study

Single subject research with multiple baseline design across behaviors was employed. The participants were exposed to a non-treatment and a treatment phase and performance is measured during each phase. Two children were subjected to the intervention and the matched pair served as the control group.

5.1.4.4 Procedure

The four children selected for the study were matched and paired based on age, date of admission to the school (duration of special care), severity of Autism Rating, and Sensory Sensitivity/ Sensory preferences, assessed using the tools mentioned above. An intervention plan with activities tailored according to their subjective needs was prepared for the two participants (experimental group). Three activities requiring motor, communicative and cognitive functioning were chosen and presented to the subject in a session.

The multiple baseline design across behaviors design begins with the concurrent measurements of two or more behaviors of the single participant. After steady state responding has been obtained under baseline conditions, the investigator applied the independent variable to one of the behaviors while maintaining baseline conditions for the other behavior(s). The multisensory stimulation view was held in choosing the activities, the way the activity was executed and providing the consequence. Over and above the research objectives, the ultimate goal was that no attempt at communication should go unnoticed by the child.

A trained psychologist also participated in the study who assessed and scored the experimental subjects during the baseline and intervention phases. An inter observer agreement was also checked for the reliability of the scoring given to the performance of the children. Posttest scores of the four subjects were done using the Sensory Index inventory after three months. The results were plotted on graphs and visually analyzed.

5.1.4.5 Analyses of Data

1. *Wilcoxon signed rank test* was done to test whether the scores of the two experimenters varied significantly for the two subjects intervened.

2. *Visual analysis* of the line graphs were plotted for the multiple baseline design and histograms were erected for showing the sensory profile of the four participants.

3. *Effect size calculation* using NAP (Non-overlap of all pairs) method.

5.2 Major Findings

It is found that the two observers agreed about the performance variation in the two participants when subjected to the study. This enhances the believability of the procedure. The finding is stated as:

- There is no significant difference between the scores assigned by the researcher and the observer for the performance of the first participant in the behavior modification program.

- There is no significant difference between the scores assigned by the researcher and the observer for the performance of the second participant in the behavior modification program.

One of the major findings of the study is that the performance level of each child improved with the multisensory stimulation. Innovative therapists have recognized the possibility that children might be more motivated in situations that contain change and novelty. The data from this investigation provide empirical documentation demonstrating that the task variations- stimulating various domains ,contingency as well as quality of the reinforcements, substantially improved the on-task behavior of children.

- The level of the target behavior of the first participant increased across baseline and treatment phases of the research design when using a multi sensory stimulation procedure.
- The level of the target behavior of the second participant increased across baseline and treatment phases of the research design

Another chief finding of the study is that the performance of the children showed improvement in level and variation in trends indicating the effectiveness of the intervention. Thus the intervention model helped to develop self-efficacy of the child and thus a better assuredness about their abilities.

- The target behavior of the first participant showed trends during baseline and treatment phases of the research design when subjected to multi sensory stimulation procedure.
- The target behavior of the second participant showed trends during baseline and treatment phases of the research design when subjected to multi sensory stimulation procedure.

There is a notable difference in the Sensory profile of the experimental group, after multi sensory stimulation procedure when compared against the control group.

The improvement noticed in the sensory indices of the experimental pair is yet another significant finding. It is well documented that children with peer interaction or communication difficulties and rigidity are more likely to engage in self-stimulatory behavior. It is concluded that the intervention was effective in reducing sensory integration dysfunction and in improving interpersonal communication skills.

Another noteworthy finding is that display of off-task (e.g., self-stimulatory) behavior produced is highly reduced when a variety of stimulations are introduced and the time gap between trials is reduced. According to Baer et al (1968) the opportunity for off task behaviors occur if there is more inter trial interval. The first participant had vestibular and proprioceptive self stimulatory behavior which significantly reduced with the intervention(vide table 11). In the case of the second participant also the self stimulatory behavior got reduced. Of note is the degree of behavioral change over the course of the study.

The overarching research question was,

- Does the use of multi sensory stimulation procedure prove effective in the management of autism?

Although interventions based on Multisensory stimulation have been proposed to work well with those with autism, there has been minimal research validating this hypothesis. By using the method in conjunction with improving intrinsic motivation strategies, and managing the outcome, this study serves to show how the approach facilitate functioning of the children subjected.

According to Watling and Dietz(2007) interventions can be effectively presented, and sensory seeking behaviors decreased once individual sensory needs have been met. When activities were designed according to the sensory needs of the children a feeling of in control aroused. In the present study, management of autism from the perspective of the therapist meant dealing an autistic person without much difficulty and helping him develop.

Visual inspection and statistical analyses of the scores indicated that the level of response of the children subjected to Multisensory stimulation went up showing marked improvement in the social functioning. The trends mostly showed hikes and stable patterns indicating "change".

The researcher could build a trustful relationship with each child. This stems from the optimal stimulation (of various modalities as an activity required), gradually escalating the complexity of goals which promotes the child to initiate actions, immediate presentation of the reinforcement, having a high regard for the approximations the child makes towards the goal and maintaining consistency of the approach. Such a scenario made the children 'adjust' - "…..an adjustment made to a stimulating condition of such a kind that involves a marked change in energy level" (Duffy,1941). It should be noted that an overall pattern of increase in the target behaviors occurred during the intervention stages; sporadic decreases were noted and could potentially be associated with illnesses experienced by the participant and some fluctuation in the professionals who were assigned to the participant. These findings help to substantiate the efficacy of the multisensory stimulation procedure in the management of autism.

5.3. Tenability of Hypotheses

Based on the findings, the hypotheses formulated for the study and presented in Chapter 1 could be re- examined to evaluate their tenability. The conclusions arrived at in this regard are presented below;

Hypothesis 1

There is significant difference between the scores assigned by the researcher and the observer for the performance of the first participant in the behavior modification program focusing on multisensory stimulation procedure.

Based on the inference drawn from Inter observer rating, hypothesis 1 is not substantiated.

Hypothesis 2

There is significant difference between the scores assigned by the researcher and the observer for the performance of the second participant in the behavior modification program focusing on multisensory stimulation procedure.

Based on the inference drawn from Inter observer rating, hypothesis 2 is not substantiated.

Hypothesis 3

The level of the target behavior of the first participant varies across baseline and treatment phases of the research design when using a multi sensory stimulation procedure.

Based on the inferences drawn from the Visual analysis of level variation in the performance of the first participant, hypothesis 3 is substantiated.

Hypothesis 4

The level of the target behavior of the second participant varies across baseline and treatment phases of the research design when using a multi sensory stimulation procedure.

On the basis of the inferences drawn from the Visual analysis of level variation in the performance of the second participant, hypothesis 4 is substantiated.

Hypothesis 5

The target behaviors of the first participant show trends during baseline and treatment phases of the research design when using a multi sensory stimulation procedure.

Based on the inferences drawn from the Visual analysis of trends in the performance of first participant, hypothesis 5 is substantiated.

Hypothesis 6

The target behaviors of the second participant show trends during baseline and treatment phases of the research design when using a multi sensory stimulation procedure.

Based on the inferences drawn from, the Visual analysis of trends in the performance of the second participant, hypothesis 6 is substantiated.

Hypothesis 7

There will be substantial difference in the Sensory profile of the experimental group, after multi sensory stimulation procedure when compared against the control group.

Based on the inferences drawn from the Visual analysis of histograms plotting the sensory profile variations in the experimental and control group, hypothesis 7 is substantiated.

5.4 Implications of the study

Theoretical implications

Well-designed single case studies are particularly appropriate where there is individual target setting, and/or where the magnitude of observed changes in children can be related to well-established relevant measures; however, for research evidence at the level required to guide broad strategies for service development, large randomized controlled trials are required. The present study shall be considered as a preliminary study shedding light into wider prospects at improving the management of autism. Ultimately, such work may provide useful clinical tool for early diagnosis and remediation.

It is essential that as practitioners, we become familiar and informed about the various evidence-based models but in most instances an integration of research findings like the one here , into "real-world" practice is more likely to occur than rigid application of existing evidence-based intervention models. The research seems to guide practitioners with regard to what approach is (likely to be) most beneficial for autistic children.

Practical implications

The implications for practice are numerous. Need for early intervention in autism is a recognized fact. As laid by Bibby, Eikeseth, Martin, Mudford, & Reeves (2002) development of parent education, parent-initiated, or parent-managed intervention programs is a method espoused for expanding services for children with ASD. Awareness building in the parents regarding the impact of stimulus variations , sensory deprivation and requirements in the child is crucial for generating long-term ability in a parent to solve newly arising day to day problems. Training is required to consider all of the potential issues that could develop (delays, noise, crowds, weather) when taking the child somewhere. Empowering the less competent parents is highly recommended with the belief that regardless of the severity or frequency of their child's difficulties, they have the ability to deal with their child effectively and are truly the experts. (Weiss, Sullivan, & Diamond, 2005).

Teachers and important others ought to understand the need for eliciting active attempts, from a child, through optimal multi sensory stimulation. The findings of the study thus have great relevance in ensuring an eventual "solution" for their concerns.

5.5 Limitations of the Study

When assessing the implications of these findings, the following limitations should be considered. Results showed various degrees of improvements in specific targeted behaviors. Some of the targeted behaviors were exhibited consistently by the end of the training period, whereas other targeted behaviors were exhibited inconsistently.

The first limitation is that this is a single case study design exploring the effectiveness of a program on behavior of autistic children. Although the two subjects showed clear improvements in their motor, communicative and cognitive skills, replicating the study with larger number of autistic children would be necessary to demonstrate generalizability of the results. A study involving a larger number of participants would allow for examination of variation in training effectiveness also. We could not effectively control history effects and generalization of results due to the demands of the research design.

Some major limitations of the study presented themselves during the course of the study. The length of data collection was not extensive enough to note a significant change in behavior during the baseline as well as following intervention. Observation of the baseline behavior as well as outcomes of intervention was limited to a three-month period during which the training was conducted, making it difficult to conclude with certainty that the behaviors would continue to be exhibited without prompting after conclusion of the training program. The host of activities assessed and intervened within a short period, limited the time scheduled for each. The drawback resulted was that the variations in the baselines could not be observed until it became stable in several instances.

The limitation mentioned above also relates to the number of data points in each phase of the graphs. Eight observations is the lower limit recommended to compute the split-middle method of trend estimation. A larger number of data points would improve the accuracy of the celeration line.

Anyone who has worked with children with autism knows that they often fail to show stimulus generalization and the present study is no exception. A therapist can teach a child a behavior in a therapy room only to find that the child will not perform the behavior for another therapist or in another room.

Several factors affect the subject's enthusiasm and/or alertness to perform consistently with expectations, as when working with different people, in different settings and different time of the day. There were some people whom the kids found very interesting and others that were of little or no interest to them. Although it was not studied systematically, it was observed by the raters that the subjects required more prompting in the settings that were not interesting to him.

The unit of analysis used in this study (the AB design) also may represent a limitation. The AB design is the basic unit of analysis in single-subject research. The AB configuration serves as the foundation for more complex multiple baseline and reversal designs. In practice, however, the simple AB design is rarely used as the functional framework to manipulate the independent variable. More complex designs, including those with several phase changes or multiple baselines may have produced different results.

Other limitations exist. Inter observer agreement in the current study was measured at only one time point. Studies examining the course of behavior change as experienced by either rater would be particularly informative.

Methodological update though highly preferred was not used in the present study. For statistical computing and graphics, latest software environment that compiles and runs on a wide variety of platforms could have given a better analysis of the result; another stalemate was the unavailability of trained professionals in this area.

5.6 Suggestions for Further Research

Our findings generated more questions than answers, and there are several ways that future investigations can build upon this study.

Since most children with severe handicaps need to receive treatment for many behaviors it is essential to identify target behaviors for treatment that will produce simultaneous changes in many other behaviors instead of having to treat each individual behavior one at a time - a task that would be prohibitively time consuming.

Teachers' lack of planning time, high student-to-staff ratio, and lack of administrative support to implement behavior changes in general have been cited as problems related to effective training. Children with ASD often have trouble generalizing and they need to be taught specific skills. If skills are taught in school and practiced at home, they will generalize more quickly. Training a behavior in the presence of a sufficient number of adults, or in a sufficient number of settings, or to a sufficient number of instructional stimuli until generalization is produced to untrained exemplars (i.e., other adults, settings, and instructional material) is also suggested.

The effective intervention for children with ASD is dependent on an understanding that the behavior of these individuals is the result of a constellation of neurobiological impairments rather than willful acts of non-compliance. Direct training in the use of the intervention techniques discussed in this study will help to facilitate the participation of these children in both the assessment and therapeutic process. There is no uniform formula to determine which of these techniques to use nor how to use them since each person brings his / her own history, caregivers, developmental potentials and personal learning characteristics. The pervasiveness of the condition demands a special kind of all embracing approach as everything we do within the curriculum affects the child's development, including the way in which we try to monitor progress.

Although further research is recommended to further validate the findings, the interventions used in this study did lead to some positive (although inconsistent) results and are recommended for use by trained professionals. It was the author's intent to provide a detailed description of the participant's behaviors and the interventions utilized in this study to help readers determine if the participant's behaviors can be generalized to that of the their own situation, allowing them to determine if they can use the same interventions, or modified versions, with their own clients, to address targeted behaviors. Although the case study has clear limitations regarding size, scope and generalizability, it offers itself as a stepping-stone for continued research into sensory stimulations and their significance.

CPSIA information can be obtained
at www.ICGtesting.com
Printed in the USA
LVHW021319031222
734485LV00013B/947